P9-CRB-948

READING AND WRITING Sourcebook

Authors
Ruth Nathan
Laura Robb

Great Source Education Group
a Houghton Mifflin Company

Authors

Ruth Nathan one of the authors of *Writers Express* and *Write Away*, is the author of many professional books and articles on literacy. She earned a Ph.D. in reading from Oakland University in Rochester, Michigan, where she co-headed their reading research laboratory for several years. She currently teaches in third grade, as well as consults with numerous schools and organizations on reading.

Laura Robb author of *Reading Strategies That Work* and *Teaching Reading in the Middle School*, has taught language arts at Powhatan School in Boyce, Virginia, for more than thirty years. She also mentors and coaches teachers in Virginia public schools and speaks at conferences throughout the country.

Copyright ©2001 by Great Source Education Group, a division of Houghton Mifflin Company. All rights reserved.

No part of this work may be reproduced or transmitted in any form or by any means, electronic or mechanical, including photocopying and recording, or by any information storage retrieval system without the prior written permission of the copyright owner unless such copying is expressly permitted by federal copyright law. With the exception of non-profit transcription in Braille, Great Source Education Group is not authorized to grant permission for further uses of copyrighted selections reprinted in this text without the permission of their owners. Permission must be obtained from the individual copyright owners as identified herein. Address requests for permission to make copies of Great Source material only to Great Source Education Group, 181 Ballardvale Street, Wilmington, MA 01887.

Great Source® is a registered trademark of Houghton Mifflin Company.

Printed in the United States of America.

International Standard Book Number -13: 978-0-669-48440-3

International Standard Book Number -10: 0-669-48440-7

8 9 10 — RRD — 07

Table of Contents

©GREAT SOURCE. COPYING IS PROHIBITED.

3

TABLE OF CONTENTS

©GREAT SOURCE. COPYING IS PROHIBITED.

Be an Active Reader

When you read, do you mark up the text? Do you write down questions about your reading? Active readers read with a pen in hand. They make notes, underline, and draw. It's easy to become an active reader.

Read 4 poems and see the examples of how one active reader took notes. You too can **draw**, **question**, **make clear**, and **connect** to the reading.

GREAT SOURCE. COPYING IS PROHIBITED.

I. DRAW

You can **draw** to help you "see" what you read. Here the reader has drawn an angel. The picture puts an image with the words in the poem.

Response Notes

EXAMPLE:

"Blossoms" by Walter Dean Myers

I never dreamt
that tender <u>blossoms</u>
Would be brown
Or precious angels
could come down
to live in the garden
of my giving heart
But here you are
brown angel

blossoms (blos•soms)—flowers.

© GREAT SOURCE. COPYING IS PROHIBITED.

QUESTION

You can ask **questions** as you read. Writing down questions—
and trying to answer them—helps you understand what you're
reading.

"Summer" by Walter Dean Myers

I like hot days, hot days
Sweat is what you got days
Bugs buzzin from cousin to cousin
Juices dripping
Running and ripping
Catch the one you love days

Birds peeping
Old men sleeping
Lazy days, daisies lay
Beaming and dreaming
Of hot days, hot days,
Sweat is what you got days

Response Notes

EXAMPLE:

Did the author have a
big family?

© GREAT SOURCE. COPYING IS PROHIBITED.

II. MAKE CLEAR

You can **make clear** what you read by writing notes. That way you know what is happening in the reading. Here the notes focus on one line. They make clear why the writer might want to hear wise thoughts.

Response Notes

EXAMPLE:

Maybe the writer thinks he can become wise.

"Prayer" by Walter Dean Myers

Shout my name to the angels
Sing my song to the skies
Anoint my ears with wisdom
Let beauty fill my eyes

For I am dark and precious
And have such gifts to give
Sweet joy, sweet love,
Sweet laughter
Sweet wondrous life to live

Anoint (a•**noint**)—rub or smear.
wondrous (won•drous)—wonderful.

© GREAT SOURCE. COPYING IS PROHIBITED.

IV. CONNECT

As you read, think about what the reading means to you. How can you **connect** it to something you've done? Here the poem is about the love of a little boy. How has the reader connected his or her own experiences to the poem?

"Love That Boy"
by Walter Dean Myers

Love that boy,
like a rabbit loves to run
I said I love that boy
like a rabbit loves to run
Love to call him in the morning
love to call him
"Hey there, son!"

He walk like his grandpa
<u>grins</u> like his uncle Ben
I said he walk like his grandpa
and grins like his uncle Ben
Grins when he happy
when he sad he grins again

grins—smiles.

Response Notes

EXAMPLE:
I like to wake up my little sister in the morning.

© GREAT SOURCE. COPYING IS PROHIBITED.

His mama like to hold him
like to feed him cherry pie
I said his mama like to hold him
feed him that cherry pie
She can have him now
I'll get him <u>by and by</u>

He got long roads to walk down,
before the setting sun
I said he got a long, long road
to walk down,
before the setting sun
He'll be a long <u>stride</u> walker
and a good man before he done

by and by—soon.
stride—big step.

G. A. Moore,   Crystal Springs,
Photographer.   Miss.

© GREAT SOURCE. COPYING IS PROHIBITED.

How to Read a Lesson

Here are 3 easy steps to help you get the most out of the readings in this book.

1. For each reading, **read it once** and just circle or underline the important parts.

2. Then **read it again**. On the second reading, write questions or comments in the Notes.

3. Then, at the end of each reading, you will find a part called **Reread**. This part asks you to go back one more time and be sure you have answered all the questions.

© GREAT SOURCE. COPYING IS PROHIBITED.

Red=Follow Directions

Blue=Write Here

Black=Read This

GEORGE WASHINGTON CARVER

READ

Read this part of *George Washington Carver*.
1. On the first time through, underline parts of the story that make you ask questions about George's life.
2. On your second reading, write the **questions** that popped into your head in the Notes.

George Washington Carver
by Patricia and Fredrick McKissack

Moses and Susan Carver owned a small farm in Diamond Grove, Missouri. They owned one slave, Mary. She had two small children, James and George.

One day a neighbor came to warn the Carvers. Slave raiders were in the area. Slave raiders stole slaves and sold them again.

The raiders came late that night. They stole Mary and baby George, and rode away. Moses Carver went after them. They found baby George by the side of the road. They never found Mary.

The Carvers had no children. So they raised James and George as their own. The boys called the Carvers Aunt Susan and Uncle Moses.

Slave raiders (slave raid•ers)—persons who stole slaves and sold them to someone else.

Response Notes

EXAMPLE:
What happened to his mom?

15

© GREAT SOURCE. COPYING IS PROHIBITED.

reread

Reread *George Washington Carver* one last time. Think about what Carver's childhood was like. Be sure you have answered all of the **Stop and Retell** questions.

18

By reading and rereading, you will do what good readers do.

How To Read a Lesson

GREAT SOURCE. COPYING IS PROHIBITED.

George Washington Carver

How would you feel if you were alone in the world? Wouldn't you be glad if someone offered to help you? George Washington Carver became a great man, even though the odds were against him.

© GREAT SOURCE. COPYING IS PROHIBITED.

I.

BEFORE YOU READ

With a partner, read the sentences below from *George Washington Carver*.

1. Decide which sentence comes first, which comes next, and so on. Number the sentences in order.
2. Talk with your partner about what the sentences made you think about. Then answer the questions below.

☐ "George wanted to go to college."

☐ "George was a sickly boy."

☐ "When George was about twelve years old, he left the Carvers."

☐ "Aunt Susan taught him to read and write."

What did these sentences make you think about?

What do you think George Washington Carver will be about?

© GREAT SOURCE. COPYING IS PROHIBITED.

MY PURPOSE

Who was George Washington Carver, and what was his childhood like?

Read this part of *George Washington Carver*.
1. On the first time through, underline parts of the story that make you ask questions about George's life.
2. On your second reading, write the **questions** that popped into your head in the Notes.

George Washington Carver
by Patricia and Fredrick McKissack

Response Notes

Moses and Susan Carver owned a small farm in Diamond Grove, Missouri. They owned one slave, Mary. She had two small children, James and George.

One day a neighbor came to warn the Carvers. <u>Slave raiders</u> were in the area. Slave raiders stole slaves and sold them again.

The raiders came late that night. They stole Mary and baby George, and rode away. Moses Carver went after them. They found baby George by the side of the road. <u>They never found Mary.</u>

The Carvers had no children. So they raised James and George as their own. The boys called the Carvers Aunt Susan and Uncle Moses.

EXAMPLE:

What happened to his mom?

Slave raiders (slave raid•ers)—persons who stole slaves and sold them to someone else.

© GREAT SOURCE. COPYING IS PROHIBITED.

Why wasn't George raised by his mother?

....

....

....

....

Response Notes

GEORGE WASHINGTON CARVER
(continued)

George was a <u>sickly</u> boy. His voice was thin and weak. He <u>stuttered</u> sometimes when he spoke in a hurry. But he was a happy child who loved plants and animals.

Aunt Susan taught him to read and write. She gave him a Bible. He loved his Bible very much.

The boy was always full of questions. He wanted to learn about everything. But the only school for black children was miles away. It was too far for a little boy to walk each day. George had to wait.

When George was about twelve years old, he left the Carvers. He wanted to go to school. He walked to Neosho, Missouri. A family found

sickly (sick•ly)—not well; often ill.
stuttered (stut•tered)—spoke while repeating and pausing between sounds.

© GREAT SOURCE. COPYING IS PROHIBITED.

16

GEORGE WASHINGTON CARVER
(continued)

George sleeping in their barn. They let the boy live with them. George worked and went to Lincoln School.

stop and retell

Why did George leave the Carvers?

A few years passed. George learned all he could at Lincoln. He heard about a school in Fort Scott, Kansas. So he moved there. Another family let George live with them. Soon, young Carver was old enough to live on his own. For a while he moved from place to place.

Then he came to a small Kansas town. Another George Carver lived there too. So George added a "W" to his name. "It is for Washington," he told his friends. *George Washington Carver*—he liked the sound of his new name.

© GREAT SOURCE. COPYING IS PROHIBITED.

George wanted to go to college. Not many black men went to college in the 1890s. But George Carver was sure that he would go. He worked hard and saved his money.

At last Carver went to college in Iowa. There he studied what he liked best—plants and farming.

STOP AND RETELL *stop and retell* **STOP AND RETELL**

What things did George do so he could go to college?

reread

Reread *George Washington Carver*. Think about what Carver's childhood was like. Be sure you have answered all of the **Stop and Retell** questions.

© GREAT SOURCE. COPYING IS PROHIBITED.

WORD WORK

You can make a long word by joining 2 small words. The long word is called a **compound word**. Here are some examples:

after + noon = *afternoon*   bean + bag = *beanbag*

1. Read each of the compound words below.
2. Then write each of the 2 smaller words in the chart. One has been done for you.

Compound Word	Small Word	Small Word
• myself	my	self
• sometimes		
• nobody		
• herself		
• grandfather		
• farmhouse		

READING TIP:
When you read a long word, ask yourself, "Is it a compound word? Can I find the two small words and say each one?" Finding small words in a long word can help you read a new word.

READING REMINDER

Asking questions while you read helps you understand what you've read and remember details.

GREAT SOURCE. COPYING IS PROHIBITED.

III. GET READY TO WRITE

A. REFLECT

Think about the story of George Washington Carver. Answer the questions below about his childhood.

1. How are strangers kind to him?

2. How do they help him along the way?

B. BRAINSTORM

Get ready to write a journal entry about a time you were kind to someone. Brainstorm about one of those times below.

What did I do?	When did it happen?	Who was there?

Where was I?	Why did I do it?	How did I feel afterward?

GREAT SOURCE. COPYING IS PROHIBITED.

IV. WRITE

Now you are ready to write your own **journal entry**.

1. Reread your brainstorm chart on page 20.
2. Explain what your kind act was, when it took place, who was there, and what happened.
3. In the last sentence, tell how you felt about doing the kind act.
4. Use the Writers' Checklist to edit your journal entry.

Date_____

Dear Journal,

GREAT SOURCE. COPYING IS PROHIBITED.

Continue writing on the next page.

Continue your journal entry.

....

....

....

....

....

....

....

....

....

WRITERS' CHECKLIST

Capitalization

☐ **Did you capitalize all proper names?** EXAMPLE: *Her name was Jennifer Katherine Dunn.*

☐ **Did you capitalize the first word in each sentence?** EXAMPLE: *He went to school.*

LOOK BACK

What part of George Washington Carver's life did you most enjoy reading about? Write your answer below.

....

....

Think about Your Reading

READERS' CHECKLIST

Enjoyment

☐ **Was the reading easy to read?**

☐ **Were you able to read it smoothly?**

© GREAT SOURCE. COPYING IS PROHIBITED.

Tornado

Imagine the wind and rain shaking
the walls of your home. Imagine
a wind so strong it rips the
roof off the house. What
would you do?

© GREAT SOURCE. COPYING IS PROHIBITED.

BEFORE YOU READ

Have you ever tried to figure out what will happen next in a story? When you do, you are using clues in the story and what you know to make a prediction.

1. Read the title and the first paragraph.
2. Next, read the 4 sentences below from the story.
3. Tell what you think *Tornado* will be about.

- "Along about lunch, it hit."
- "The doghouse was trembling."
- "I brought him water, but he wouldn't drink."
- "I said, 'Daddy, can we keep him?'"

My prediction: I predict this story will be about

MY PURPOSE

What happens during the tornado, and is everyone okay?

© GREAT SOURCE. COPYING IS PROHIBITED.

READ

Do you ever "see" what is happening as you read? Read this part of *Tornado* and make pictures in your mind of the action, characters, and setting.

1. On your first reading, circle parts that help you see a character or scene.
2. Read *Tornado* a second time. In the Notes, **draw** sketches of what you see.

Tornado by Betsy Byars

At breakfast that morning, I remember my mother looked up from the stove, took a breath, and said, "I smell a storm."

I <u>shivered</u> a little, because my mother's nose was always right.

My daddy said, "Well, you kids better stay close to the house."

The morning went by, slow and scary. We did stay close to the house. Folks didn't call our part of the country *Tornado Alley* for nothing.

Along about lunch, it hit. Only there was no warning like we had

shivered (shiv•ered)—shook.

Response Notes

EXAMPLE:

© GREAT SOURCE. COPYING IS PROHIBITED.

today. No <u>funnel cloud</u>, no nothing. One minute we were eating beans and <u>biscuits</u> at the table. Next there was a roar—worse than a train— worse than a hundred trains. And then there came a terrible tearing sound, like the world was being ripped apart. I can still hear it in my mind.

I looked up, and I saw sky. The ceiling was clean gone. There was the sky! The tornado had torn the roof off the kitchen and left the food on the table and us in our seats.

My daddy was the first to be able to speak. He said, "Well, I'm surprised to find myself alive."

That was how we all felt. We looked at our arms and legs to make sure they were still hooked on us.

funnel cloud (**fun•**nel **cloud**)—cone-shaped cloud that sweeps over the land during a tornado.
biscuits (**bis•**cuits)—soft bread or dough that is baked.

© GREAT SOURCE. COPYING IS PROHIBITED.

Response Notes

Then my father pushed back his chair and said, "Let's go see the <u>damage</u>."

DOUBLE-ENTRY JOURNAL

Quote	What You Think This Means
"We looked at our arms and legs to make sure they were still hooked on us."	

Outside, the yard was not our yard anymore. The tree with the tire swing was laid flat. The tops of all the pine trees had been snapped off. A doghouse I had never seen before was beside the well. A piece of bicycle was here, the hood of a car there. I stepped over somebody's clothesline that still had some clothes on it.

The roof of the kitchen lay at the edge of the garden. It was folded

damage (dam•age)—harm or injury done to something.

© GREAT SOURCE. COPYING IS PROHIBITED.

Response Notes

shut like a book. We walked
over there.

"It was about time for a new roof,"
my daddy said. He always tried to
find the good in something.

DOUBLE-ENTRY JOURNAL

Quote	What You Think This Means
"He always tried to find the good in something."	

I was just walking around,
looking at other people's things,
when I heard a rattling noise.

I kept listening and looking, and
finally I realized the sound was
coming from that doghouse. I went
over to it.

The doghouse was <u>trembling</u>. You
could see it. It was trembling. It was
shaking. It was doing everything but
having a fit.

trembling (trem•bling)—shaking slightly.

© GREAT SOURCE. COPYING IS PROHIBITED.

I looked inside, and there was a big black dog. He was <u>panting</u> so hard, I could feel his breath. He was shaking so hard, the doghouse was in danger of losing its boards.

"Daddy, there's a dog in here!"

My daddy came over.

"Look, Daddy. It's a big black dog."

My daddy leaned down and took a look.

"Well, you can come on out now," he told the dog. "The storm's over, and you're among friends."

panting (pant•ing)—breathing hard.

DOUBLE-ENTRY JOURNAL

Quote	What You Think This Means
"'The storm's over, and you're among friends.'"	

© GREAT SOURCE. COPYING IS PROHIBITED.

The dog just kept shaking.

"Maybe I can pull him out," I said.

"Don't you put your hand in there," my mother said.

"Yes, leave him be, Pete."

All that day, all that night, all the next day that dog shook. I brought him water, but he wouldn't drink. I brought him food, but he wouldn't eat.

Then that night my mother leaned out the kitchen door and yelled, "Supper!" as she usually did. The dog heard her and stuck his head out of the doghouse. He must have been <u>familiar</u> with the word.

familiar (fa•mil•iar)—having knowledge of; acquainted.

DOUBLE-ENTRY JOURNAL

Quote	What You Think This Means
"He must have been familiar with the word."	

© GREAT SOURCE. COPYING IS PROHIBITED.

Response Notes

He came out, stood there, looked around for a moment, and then gave one final shake, as if he were shaking off the past.

Then he came over and joined us at the back door.

I said, "Daddy, can we keep him? Please?"

"If we don't find the owner."

"Can we call him Tornado?"

"Until we find the owner."

"We'll have to ask around," my mother reminded me.

"I know."

My daddy bent down. "Let's see what kind of manners you got, Tornado. Shake!"

reread

Reread *Tornado*. Think about what happened during the storm. Be sure to write what you think the quotes mean in the **Double-entry Journals.**

© GREAT SOURCE. COPYING IS PROHIBITED.

WORD WORK

Words have beats—1, 2, 3, or more beats. Try clapping *stolen*. You clapped 2 times because *sto•len* has 2 beats called **syllables**. Dividing words into syllables can make them easier to say and read.

Some words with 2 syllables have consonant letters in the middle. These letters can be the same (*hap•py*). The letters can be 2 different consonants (*mor•ning*).

WORD BOX

border	stutter	questions	manners	artist	college

1. Put the words with the same consonant letters in the middle in the left-hand column.
2. Put the words with 2 different consonant letters in the middle in the right-hand column.
3. Put a line between the consonants to divide each word. One has been done for you.

Same Consonant Letters	Different Consonant Letters
	bor/der

© GREAT SOURCE. COPYING IS PROHIBITED.

READING REMINDER

Making pictures in your head—or visualizing the people, places, and action in a story—helps you understand and remember the story.

III. GET READY TO WRITE

A. BRAINSTORM

Get ready to write a letter to a friend about a pet you have or would like to have. Brainstorm a list of ideas about the pet.

1. Use the web below to organize your ideas about pets.

2. Study the examples and then add your own answers to each question.

What does the pet look like?

furry

How do you care for a pet?

give it food

My Pet

What can a pet do for you?

What makes a good pet?

© GREAT SOURCE. COPYING IS PROHIBITED.

B. LOOK AT A MODEL

Here are the 5 parts of a friendly letter. Use the model to help you write your own letter.

1. date

September 22, 2000

2. greeting

Dear Pedro,

3. body

You'll never guess what happened today! I found a pet. It's a small white dog. I feed him, and he makes me very happy.

4. closing

Your friend,

5. signature

Alicia M. Storm

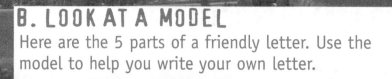

© GREAT SOURCE. COPYING IS PROHIBITED.

IV. WRITE

Now you are ready to write your own **letter**.

1. Reread your notes from page 33 and review the parts of a friendly letter.
2. Begin by talking about the pet you have or want.
3. Then write about what you can do for the pet and what the pet can do for you.
4. Close with a sentence that tells why this pet is (or will be) a great friend.
5. Use the Writers' Checklist to edit your letter.

Continue writing on the next page.

©GREAT SOURCE. COPYING IS PROHIBITED

Continue your letter.

....

....

....

....

....

....

....

....

WRITERS' CHECKLIST

Letters

☐ **Did you capitalize each word of the greeting and put a comma after the last word?**

EXAMPLE: *Dear Nora,*

☐ **Did you capitalize only the first word in the closing and use a comma at the end?**

EXAMPLE: *Yours truly,*

☐ **Did you put a comma between the day of the month and the year?**

EXAMPLE: *Dec. 18, 2000*

V. LOOK BACK

What made *Tornado* easy to read? What made it hard to read? Write your ideas below.

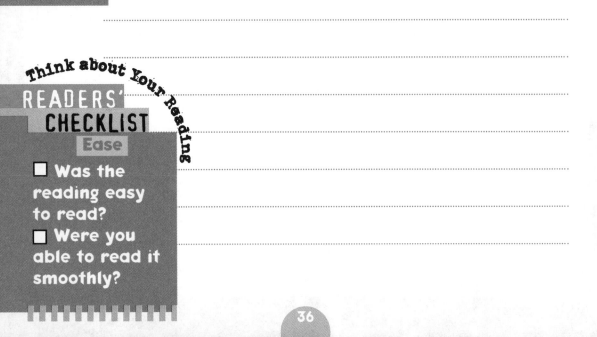

....

Think about Your Reading

READERS' CHECKLIST

Ease

☐ **Was the reading easy to read?**

☐ **Were you able to read it smoothly?**

....

....

....

© GREAT SOURCE. COPYING IS PROHIBITED.

Baseball Saved Us

In the 1940s, the United States was at war with Japan. War scares people and sometimes makes them do things they regret. The American government made Japanese people living in the United States stay in prisons called internment camps. The government took away their homes, jobs, and happiness.

GREAT SOURCE. COPYING IS PROHIBITED.

BEFORE YOU READ

Get ready to read *Baseball Saved Us*. Read each sentence below.
1. If you agree with a sentence, put a check (√).
2. If you disagree with a sentence, put an X.

_____ People who are born in other countries aren't real Americans.

_____ Kids can be mean to one another.

_____ Living in a prison is easy.

_____ Games can help people feel better.

_____ It is okay to do anything to your enemy during a war.

3. Now share and discuss your answers with your reading partner. Talk about what you think this reading will be about.

MY PURPOSE

What happened to Japanese Americans during the war?

GREAT SOURCE. COPYING IS PROHIBITED.

READ

Read this part of *Baseball Saved Us*.
1. On your first reading, underline facts about what life in the camps was like.
2. On your next reading, write comments in the Notes that **make clear** what you think about these facts.

Baseball Saved Us
by Ken Mochizuki

One day, my dad looked out at the endless desert and decided then and there to build a baseball field.

He said people needed something to do in Camp. We weren't in a camp that was fun, like summer camp. Ours was in the middle of nowhere, and we were behind a barbed-wire fence. Soldiers with guns made sure we stayed there, and the man in the tower saw everything we did, no matter where we were.

As Dad began walking over the dry, cracked dirt, I asked him again why we were here.

"Because," he said, "America is at war with Japan, and the government thinks that Japanese Americans can't be trusted. But it's wrong that we're in here. We're Americans too!"

Response Notes

EXAMPLE:

This is like a horrible prison.

© GREAT SOURCE. COPYING IS PROHIBITED.

Then he made a mark in the dirt and <u>mumbled</u> something about where the <u>infield</u> bases should be.

stop and think

Why are the Japanese Americans in the camp?

Back in school, before Camp, I was shorter and smaller than the rest of the kids. I was always the last to be picked for any team when we played games. Then, a few months ago, it got even worse. The kids started to call me names and nobody talked to me, even though I didn't do anything bad. At the same time the radio kept talking about some place far away called <u>Pearl Harbor</u>.

mumbled (mum•bled)—spoke with the lips closed.
infield (in•field)—playing area of a baseball field, inside the four bases.
Pearl Harbor (Pearl Har•bor)—U.S. naval base in Hawaii that was bombed by Japan in 1941, causing the United States to enter World War II.

© GREAT SOURCE. COPYING IS PROHIBITED.

BASEBALL SAVED US (continued)

One day Mom and Dad came to get me out of school. Mom cried a lot because we had to move out of our house real fast, throwing away a lot of our stuff. A bus took us to a place where we had to live in horse stalls. We stayed there for a while until we came here.

This Camp wasn't anything like home. It was so hot in the daytime and so cold at night. Dust storms came and got sand in everything, and nobody could see a thing. We sometimes got caught outside, standing in line to eat or to go to the bathroom. We had to use the bathroom with everybody else, instead of one at a time like at home.

We had to eat with everybody else, too, but my big brother Teddy ate with his own friends. We lived with a lot of people in what were called barracks. The place was small and had no walls. Babies cried at night and kept us up.

© GREAT SOURCE. COPYING IS PROHIBITED.

How does the author feel about living
in the camp?

Response Notes

BASEBALL SAVED US (continued)

Back home, the older people were
always busy working. But now, all
they did was stand or sit around.
Once Dad asked Teddy to get him a
cup of water.

"Get it yourself," Teddy said.

"What did you say?" Dad
snapped back.

The older men stood up and
pointed at Teddy. "How dare you talk
to your father like that!" one of them
shouted.

Teddy got up, kicked the crate he
was sitting on, and walked away. I
had never heard Teddy talk to Dad
that way before.

That's when Dad knew we needed
baseball. We got shovels and started
digging up the sagebrush in a big

© GREAT SOURCE. COPYING IS PROHIBITED.

BASEBALL SAVED US (continued)

empty space near the barracks. The man in the tower watched us the whole time. Pretty soon, other grown-ups and their kids started to help. We didn't have anything we needed for baseball, but the grown-ups were pretty smart. They <u>funnelled</u> water from <u>irrigation</u> ditches to flood what would become our baseball field. The water packed down the dirt and made it hard. There weren't any trees, but they found wood to build the bleachers. Bats, balls and gloves arrived in cloth sacks from friends back home. My mom and other moms took the covers off matresses and used them to make uniforms. They looked almost like the real thing.

funnelled (fun•nelled)—poured liquid into a small area using something with a wide top and a narrow bottom.
irrigation (ir•ri•ga•tion)—a system of pipes, canals, and ditches for supplying water.

reread

Reread *Baseball Saved Us*. Look at the facts you underlined about what life in the camps was like. Be sure that you have answered all of the **Stop and Think** questions.

© GREAT SOURCE. COPYING IS PROHIBITED.

WORD WORK

If you can read 1 word, it's easy to read a word that's almost the same.

Say *ball*. Now take off the *b* and put *st* in front of *all*. The new word is *stall*.

Use the letters in the box to build new words. These letters are single consonants (such as *b*, *t*, or *s*) or consonant clusters (such as *gr* or *fl*).

LETTER BOX

gr b fl st m r fr s cl ch t

1. Make 3 new words for each word listed below. You may use letters more than once.
2. One has been done for you.

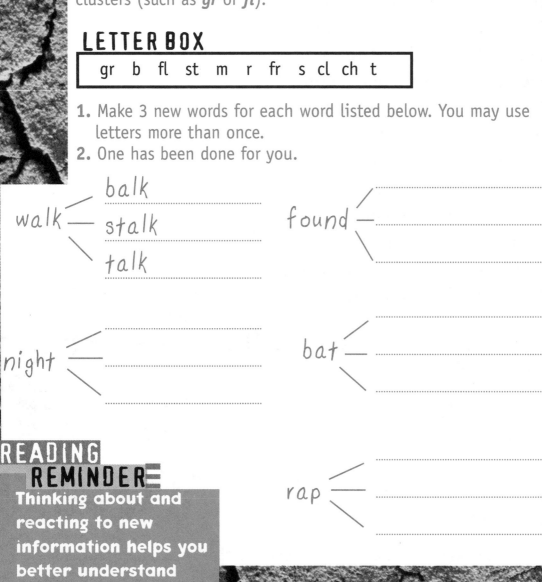

walk — balk / stalk / talk

found —

night —

bat —

rap —

READING REMINDER

Thinking about and reacting to new information helps you better understand what you read.

GREAT SOURCE. COPYING IS PROHIBITED.

III. GET READY TO WRITE

A. ORGANIZE EVENTS

Like fiction, nonfiction often tells a story. Use the storyboard below to retell the important events in *Baseball Saved Us*.

1. Put the events in the order they happened.

2. Write a different event in each box.

1. America was at war with the Japanese.

2.

3.

4.

GREAT SOURCE. COPYING IS PROHIBITED.

B. PLAN

Many people believe that the U.S. government was wrong to make the Japanese Americans go to internment camps.

1. Get ready to write a paragraph about a time when someone taught you right from wrong.
2. Answer the questions below to help you organize your paragraph.

• Who helped teach you right from wrong?

• How old were you?

• What happened?

• How did the experience end?

• How did you feel about what happened?

GREAT SOURCE. COPYING PROHIBITED.

IV. WRITE

Now you are ready to write your own **narrative paragraph** about a time someone taught you right from wrong.

1. Begin with a title. Write a topic sentence that tells what you did and when you did it.

2. Write 3 sentences in time order that tell about what happened.

3. Finish your paragraph with a closing sentence that tells how you feel about the experience.

4. Use the Writers' Checklist to edit your paragraph.

Title: ....

....

....

....

....

....

....

....

....

....

....

....

Continue writing on the next page.

GREAT SOURCE. COPYING IS PROHIBITED.

Continue your paragraph.

....

....

....

....

....

....

....

WRITERS'
CHECKLIST

Confusing Word Pairs

☐ **Did you correctly use the words *it's* (it is) and *its*?** EXAMPLES: *The dog hurt its tail. She said that it's going to rain.*

☐ **Did you correctly use the words there, their, and they're (they are)?** EXAMPLES: *The grown-ups built the field over there. The family lost all of their things. When the field is finished, they're going to play baseball.*

LOOK BACK

How did learning about what happened to the Japanese Americans during World War II make you feel? Write your answer below.

....

....

Think about Your Reading

....

....

....

READERS'
CHECKLIST

Meaning

☐ **Did you learn something from the reading?**
☐ **Did you have a strong feeling about one part of the reading?**

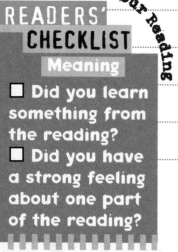

© GREAT SOURCE. COPYING IS PROHIBITED.

Feathers and The Hurricane

What does a poem mean? Poets write poems for a lot of different reasons—to explore ideas, to express an emotion, or to have fun with words. When you read a poem, think first about what the poem says to you.

© GREAT SOURCE. COPYING IS PROHIBITED.

BEFORE YOU READ

One word or idea can be very important to a poem. Making a web can help you better understand what the word or idea means. Here you'll read two poems about the wind.

1. With a partner, discuss the word *wind*. What does it mean to you? What does it mean to your partner?
2. List words or phrases that you think of when you hear the word *wind*.
3. Write your ideas on the web.

How does it feel?

What does it sound like?

Wind

What does it look like?

How does it smell or taste?

GREAT SOURCE. COPYING IS PROHIBITED.

MY PURPOSE

What do you know about the wind? How do you feel about it?

READ

Read "Feathers" and "The Hurricane."

1. First read the poems out loud to a reading partner. Then listen as your partner reads to you.

2. On the second reading, circle parts of the poems that **connect** to your feelings and experiences. Jot down your thoughts about the poem in the Notes.

"Feathers" by Joseph Bruchac

Everything that lives
wants to fly,
a <u>Mohawk</u> friend
said to me
one winter afternoon
as we watched
grosbeaks take seeds,
<u>fluttering</u> close
to our eyes.

Mohawk (Mo•hawk)—one Native American tribe.
grosbeaks (gros•beaks)—birds with conelike beaks.
fluttering (flut•ter•ing)—flapping wings quickly.

Response Notes

EXAMPLE:

Once I fed the ducks with my sister. They came right up to our feet to eat.

© GREAT SOURCE. COPYING IS PROHIBITED.

Those were
dinosaurs once,
he said,
but they
made a <u>bargain</u>.
They gave up
that power
in return for
the Sky.

bargain (bar•gain)—deal between two sides about payment or trade.

DOUBLE-ENTRY JOURNAL

Quote	What You Think This Means
"Everything that lives wants to fly."	

© GREAT SOURCE. COPYING IS PROHIBITED.

"The Hurricane"
by Ashley Bryan

Response Notes

I cried to the wind,
"Don't blow so hard!
You've knocked down my sister
You're shaking
And tossing and tilting
The tree!"

And would the wind listen,
Listen to me?

The wind howled,
"Whooree!
I blow as I wish
I wish
I wish
I crush and
I splash and
I rush and
I swish."

© GREAT SOURCE. COPYING IS PROHIBITED.

I cried to the wind,
"Don't blow so wild!
You're chasing the clouds
You're whirling
And swishing and swirling
The sea!"

DOUBLE-ENTRY JOURNAL

Quote	What You Think This Means
' "Don't blow so wild! You're chasing the clouds.' "	

And would the wind listen,
Listen to me?

The wind howled,
"Whooree!
I blow as I wish
I wish
I wish
I'm <u>bold</u> and
I'm <u>brash</u> and

bold—having no fear.
brash—likely to act quickly, without thinking about others.

© GREAT SOURCE. COPYING IS PROHIBITED.

"THE HURRICANE" (continued)

I'm cold and
I'm <u>rash</u>!"

I said to my friends,
"Please, call out with me,
Stop, wind, stop!"
        "STOP, WIND, STOP!"

Ah, *now* the wind listens
It brushes my hair
Chases clouds slowly
Sings in my ear,
"Whooree, whooree!"
Stretches out gently
Under the tree
Soothes little sister
And quiets the sea.

rash—hasty; not stopping
    to think.

reread

Reread "Feathers" and "The Hurricane" one more time. As you
read, think about how you feel about the wind. Be sure to
respond to all of the quotes in the **Double-entry Journals.**

© GREAT SOURCE. COPYING IS PROHIBITED.

WORD WORK

Knowing how to break words into syllables can make it easier to read words. When you say a word, it can have 1, 2, 3, 4, or more beats. Each beat is called a **syllable**. Try clapping out the word *wind*. You clapped once, so *wind* has 1 syllable. Try clapping *hurricane*. You clapped 3 times, so *hur•ri•cane* has 3 syllables.

1. Say and clap each word in the WORD BOX below.
2. Write each word under the correct heading.

WORD BOX

tossing	brash	afternoon	bargain	
friend	dinosaurs	power	tree	listen

1 Syllable	2 Syllables	3 Syllables

READING REMINDER

Making personal connections to a poem can help you better understand it.

© GREAT SOURCE. COPYING IS PROHIBITED.

III. GET READY TO WRITE

A. GATHER IDEAS

Most poems contain many sensory details—smell, touch, taste, hearing, sight.

1. With a reading partner, reread the poem "The Hurricane" out loud to each other.
2. Complete the chart below by saying what sensory detail is being used. One example has been done for you.

Detail	Comes from the sense of
• "You're shaking"	sight or touch
• "The wind howled"	
• "It brushes my hair"	
• "I splash and I rush and I swish."	
• "Chases clouds slowly"	

© GREAT SOURCE. COPYING IS PROHIBITED.

B. BRAINSTORM

Get ready to write your own poem about the wind.

1. Brainstorm your ideas on the cluster below.

2. Try to think of 2–3 ideas for each question.

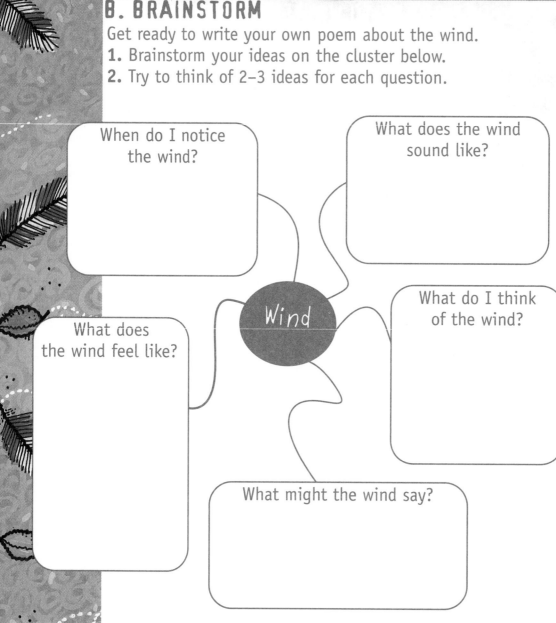

When do I notice the wind?

What does the wind sound like?

Wind

What does the wind feel like?

What do I think of the wind?

What might the wind say?

Helped by the Wind

The wind pushes me and my bike up the hill.

It sounds like a roar in my ears.

It feels cold.

"Hold onto your hat," shouts the wind.

The cool wind is my friend.

C. USE A MODEL

Read the poem to the left.

1. Note that the poem has 5 lines. Each line is based on details from one of the boxes above.

2. Use it as a model when you write a poem of your own.

© GREAT SOURCE. COPYING IS PROHIBITED.

WRITE

Now you are ready to write a **poem** about the wind.

1. Use your notes and the model on page 58 to help you.

2. Make your poem 5 lines long.

3. Give your poem a title.

4. Use the Writers' Checklist to edit your poem.

Title:

Continue writing on the next page.

© GREAT SOURCE. COPYING IS PROHIBITED.

Continue your poem.

....

....

....

....

....

....

....

....

....

WRITERS' CHECKLIST

Commas

☐ **Did you use a comma to separate items or actions listed in a series?**

EXAMPLE:
The wind feels cruel, icy, and strong.

V. LOOK BACK

What did reading "Feathers" and "The Hurricane" mean to you?
Write some of your ideas below.

....

....

....

....

....

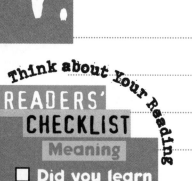

Think about Your Reading

READERS' CHECKLIST

Meaning

☐ **Did you learn something from the reading?**

☐ **Did you have a strong feeling about one part of the reading?**

© GREAT SOURCE. COPYING IS PROHIBITED.

5

Ant Cities

When there is a big job to finish, have you ever tried starting with a little job? Isn't it easier to face a big project if you break it into little parts? That's what ants do.

© GREAT SOURCE. COPYING IS PROHIBITED.

I.

BEFORE YOU READ

How can you get ready to read? One way is to ask yourself, "What do I already know about this topic?"

1. Create a web that shows what you know about ants.
2. In the circles, write words, phrases, and pictures that come to mind when you think of ants.
3. Share your web with your partner.

WHAT ARE ANTS LIKE?

WHAT DO ANTS LOOK LIKE?

HOW DO ANTS ACT?
can carry
big things

WHERE DO YOU SEE ANTS?

HOW DO YOU FEEL ABOUT ANTS?

MY PURPOSE
How do ants live and work?

©GREAT SOURCE. COPYING IS PROHIBITED.

READ

Read this part of *Ant Cities*.
1. As you read it the first time, underline parts that make a picture in your mind.
2. On your next reading, in the Notes, **draw** sketches of what you see.

Ant Cities by Arthur Dorros

Have you seen ants busy running over a hill of dirt? They may look like they are just running around. But the ants built that hill to live in, and each ant has work to do.

Some ants may <u>disappear</u> into a <u>small hole in the hill. The hole is the door to their nest.</u>

These are harvester ants. Their nest is made of lots of rooms and tunnels. These little insects made them all.

Underneath the hill there may be miles of tunnels and hundreds of rooms. The floors are <u>worn</u> smooth by thousands of ant feet. It is dark inside the nest. But the ants stay <u>cozy</u>.

disappear (dis•ap•pear)—leave your sight.
worn—damaged because of rubbing or scraping.
cozy (co•zy)—warm and snug.

Response Notes

EXAMPLE:

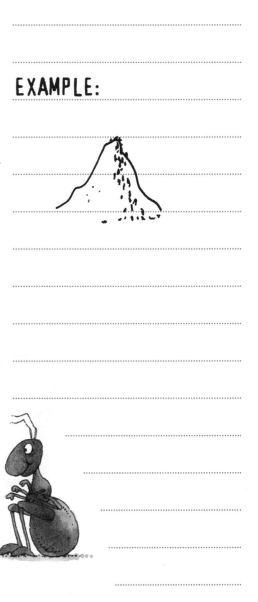

© GREAT SOURCE. COPYING IS PROHIBITED.

What have you learned about an ant nest?

....

....

....

Response Notes

ANT CITIES (continued)

In the rooms of the nest, worker ants do many different kinds of work. It is like a city, a busy city of ants.

Some ants have brought in food to the ant city. These harvester ants like seeds.

A worker ant cracks the <u>husks</u> off the seeds. Another worker will take the husks outside to throw away.

The ants chew the seeds to get the juices out. Then they feed the juices to the other ants.

husks—dry, leaflike outer coverings for corn, nuts, and seeds.

© GREAT SOURCE. COPYING IS PROHIBITED.

ANT CITIES (continued)

Other workers <u>store</u> seeds for the ants to eat another time.

Not all ants store food. But harvester ants do.

stop and think

What details have you learned about harvester ants?

In one room of the nest, a queen ant lays eggs. Workers carry the eggs away to other rooms to take care of them.

Each ant city has to have at least one queen. Without a queen there would be no ant city. All the other ants in the ant city grow from the eggs the queen lays.

At first the tiny eggs grow into <u>larvae</u>. The worker ants feed the larvae and lick them clean so they will grow well.

store—keep; put away.
larvae (lar•vae)—insects in early stage of development; wormlike creatures before they grow.

© GREAT SOURCE. COPYING IS PROHIBITED.

The larvae grow into <u>pupae</u>. The workers keep grooming the pupae until they grow into adults.

The queen ant lays thousands and thousands of eggs. Most of the eggs grow into worker ants. There may be only one queen ant in an ant city, but there can be many thousands of workers.

pupae (pu•pae)—insects in second stage of development, before they turn into the final form.

STOP AND THINK stop and think STOP AND THINK

What have you learned about how an egg grows into an ant?

STOP AND THINK STOP AND THINK STOP AND THINK

reread

Reread *Ant Cities*. Pay attention to the facts about how ants live and work. As you read, be sure to answer all of the **Stop and Think** questions.

© GREAT SOURCE. COPYING IS PROHIBITED.

WORD WORK

A **prefix** is part of a word added to the beginning of a word. A **suffix** is part of a word added to the end of a word. Prefixes and suffixes make words longer. They can also change a word's meaning.

1. Make long words by adding prefixes and suffixes to words called **base words**.
2. One has been done for you.

Prefix	+	Base Word	+	Suffix	=	New, Long Word
dis	+	appear	+	ed	=	disappeared
re	+	appear	+	ance	=	
		appear	+	ing	=	
in	+	differ	+	ent	=	
		differ	+	ence	=	
		differ	+	ent	=	

READING TIP:
Finding the base word in a long word helps you say the long word. To do this, take off the prefix and suffix and say the base word. Then put all the parts together and say the long word.

READING REMINDER

When reading about new things, picturing ideas in your mind can help you remember new facts.

© GREAT SOURCE. COPYING IS PROHIBITED

GET READY TO WRITE

FIND SUPPORTING DETAILS

When you read nonfiction, look for the main idea. That's the big point the writer is trying to make.

1. Below is the main idea of *Ant Cities*.
2. In the boxes, write facts that support the main idea. You will use these details to write a paragraph about how ants work together.

MAIN IDEA:

Ants work together to build and keep up their cities.

FACT #1

Each ant has a specific job to do.

FACT #2

Harvester ants

FACT #3

Worker ants

FACT #4

Queen ants

© GREAT SOURCE. COPYING IS PROHIBITED.

IV. WRITE

Now write an **expository paragraph** about how ants work together. Give your paragraph a title.

1. Begin with the main idea from page 68. It is your topic sentence.
2. Give 3 details that support your topic sentence.
3. End with a closing sentence that restates your main idea.
4. Use the Writers' Checklist to help you edit your paragraph.

Title:

_____

_____

_____

_____

_____

_____

_____

_____

_____

_____

_____

_____

_____

_____

_____

_____

_____

Continue writing on the next page.

© GREAT SOURCE. COPYING IS PROHIBITED.

Continue your paragraph.

....

....

....

....

....

....

....

....

WRITERS' CHECKLIST

Spelling

☐ **Did you check that you spelled all the words correctly? You may want to ask a partner to help you check words you're not sure about.**

V. LOOK BACK

What facts did you learn about ants? Write 3 facts you learned below.

....

....

....

....

....

....

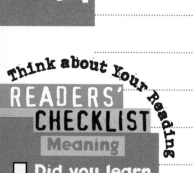

Think about Your Reading

READERS' CHECKLIST

Meaning

☐ **Did you learn something from the reading?**

☐ **Did you have a strong feeling about one part of the reading?**

© GREAT SOURCE. COPYING IS PROHIBITED.

6

Easter Parade

Not knowing about the future can be scary. Have you ever worried a lot about something? Sometimes, the best thing is to go on with your life and try not to worry about the future.

© GREAT SOURCE. COPYING IS PROHIBITED.

I.

Previewing lets you think about parts of a story before you read it. Here's how you do it.

1. Read the title and the first and last paragraphs of *Easter Parade*.
2. Look quickly through the story. Look for names and places, repeated words, and key events.
3. Finally, answer the questions below.

PREVIEWING QUESTIONS

1. Where does the story take place?

2. Who are the main characters in the story?

3. What do you think this story is about?

MY PURPOSE

Who is Elizabeth, and why are she and her mother worried?

© GREAT SOURCE. COPYING IS PROHIBITED.

I. READ

Read this part of *Easter Parade*.

1. On your first reading, underline parts of the story that **connect** to your feelings and experiences.
2. On your next reading, jot down your reactions and feelings in the Notes.

Easter Parade by Eloise Greenfield

In a red-brick <u>rowhouse</u> on a long street in Washington, D.C., Elizabeth hears the phone, but she doesn't look at it. She looks at her mother. Her mother's eyes are frightened.

Elizabeth's fingers tighten around the picture she is holding in her lap, a picture of her father in his Army <u>uniform</u>. <u>He is far away, fighting in the war.</u> She and her

rowhouse (row•house)—one of a series of houses that are side by side. They look the same and have common walls.
uniform (u•ni•form)—outfit.

Response Notes

EXAMPLE:

My uncle is also in the Army.

© GREAT SOURCE. COPYING IS PROHIBITED.

mother have been talking about missing him, and about his letters that used to come almost every day and now have stopped coming. They have been telling each other that he is all right, that no one will call on the phone to say that he has been hurt.

Her mother catches a breath and reaches for the phone.

"Hello?" she says. Her voice <u>trembles</u>. She listens, then smiles and speaks to Leanna.

"Hi, baby," she says. "How are you?" She listens again, then says, "That's good. Okay, here she is." She hands the phone to Elizabeth.

trembles (trem•bles)—shakes.

© GREAT SOURCE. COPYING IS PROHIBITED.

EASTER PARADE (continued)

Response Notes

"Hi, Leanna," Elizabeth says.

"Do you know about the parade?" Leanna asks.

"What parade?"

"The Easter parade!" Leanna says. "You're going to have one, and I'm going to have one, too."

"Oh, I know," Elizabeth says. She tries to sound excited to make her little cousin happy. "It's going to be fun."

STOP AND RETELL stop and retell STOP AND RETELL

Why are Elizabeth and her mother scared when the phone rings?

STOP AND RETELL STOP AND RETELL STOP AND RETELL

"Mama's going to sew me a new dress so I can go to it," Leanna says. "You going to it?"

"I think so," Elizabeth says.

"Okay. Guess what, I know a new joke!" Leanna says. "You wanna hear it?"

© GREAT SOURCE. COPYING IS PROHIBITED.

Leanna starts one of her too-long jokes, making it up as she goes along, and Elizabeth gets tickled and really laughs. She forgets about her worry. When she hands the phone to her mother, she is still laughing.

She watches as her mother talks to Leanna's mother, two sisters who love each other.

"No," her mother is saying, "no letter yet. It's been more than three weeks now."

She puts her mouth close to the phone and talks so quietly that Elizabeth can't understand the

© GREAT SOURCE. COPYING IS PROHIBITED.

EASTER PARADE (continued)

Response Notes

words. Then her mother stops talking and listens, and her eyes are shiny with tears.

"You're right," she says. "A letter will come. Maybe tomorrow." In a few moments, she is laughing, her eyes still wet. Her sister has said something funny.

STOP AND RETELL **stop and retell** **STOP AND RETELL**

Why does Elizabeth's mother cry?

© GREAT SOURCE. COPYING IS PROHIBITED.

STOP AND RETELL STOP AND RETELL STOP AND RETELL

When she hangs up the phone, she turns to look at Elizabeth. She asks a question with her eyes. "Do we want to have Easter?" her eyes say.

"I think Daddy wants us to," Elizabeth says.

Her mother nods. "We can't buy new clothes this year, you know. We've been sending money to Grandma."

"I know," Elizabeth says. "That's okay."

STOP AND RETELL stop and retell STOP AND RETELL

Why do Elizabeth and her mother decide to celebrate Easter?

STOP AND RETELL STOP AND RETELL STOP AND RETELL

reread

Reread *Easter Parade*. Think about how the father being gone makes Elizabeth and her mother feel. Be sure to answer all of the **Stop and Retell** questions.

© GREAT SOURCE. COPYING IS PROHIBITED.

WORD WORK

You can take 2 words and make them into 1 new word.

have not = *haven't*   we are = *we're*
will not = *won't*   we will = *we'll*

We call these new shortened words **contractions**. The apostrophe (') takes the place of the missing letter(s).
1. Write the contraction for each set of words below.
2. Make sure you use an apostrophe (') to take the place of the missing letter(s).

Words	Contraction
does not	
it is	
that is	
they will	
you are	
did not	
she will	

READING REMINDER

Previewing can connect you to a story by giving you time to think about it before you read.

© GREAT SOURCE. COPYING IS PROHIBITED.

GET READY TO WRITE

CREATE A SETTING

Elizabeth and her mother are getting ready to have Easter. Which special day do you most enjoy?

1. Write your favorite holiday below.

2. Write at least 2 words to describe it in each of the 5 sense boxes.

My favorite holiday:

DESCRIPTIVE WORDS AND PHRASES

Sound

Sight

Taste

Touch

Smell

© GREAT SOURCE. COPYING IS PROHIBITED.

WRITE

Write a **descriptive paragraph** about your favorite holiday.

1. Begin with a topic sentence that tells what and when it is.
2. Include 3–4 sensory details from page 80 that describe the special day.
3. Write a closing sentence that tells how you feel when the special day is over.
4. Use the Writers' Checklist to edit your paragraph.

Title:

© GREAT SOURCE. COPYING IS PROHIBITED.

Continue writing on the next page.

Continue your paragraph.

....

....

....

....

....

....

....

....

....

WRITERS' CHECKLIST

Contractions

■ **Did you use apostrophes correctly in all contractions? Remember that an apostrophe takes the place of a letter or letters that have been taken out.** EXAMPLES:
you + have = you▯ve
you + are = you▯re
do + not = don▯t

V. LOOK BACK

What parts of *Easter Parade* did you find the hardest to read? Why? Write your answer below.

....

....

....

....

....

....

....

Think about Your Reading

READERS' CHECKLIST

Ease

■ **Was the reading easy to read?**
■ **Were you able to read it smoothly?**

© GREAT SOURCE. COPYING IS PROHIBITED.

7

Vanished!
The Mysterious Disappearance of
Amelia Earhart

Follow your dreams. Reach for the highest star. Try, try again. Has anyone ever said these things to you? Sometimes you have to change the way other people think in order to follow your dream. That's what Amelia Earhart did when she became a pilot.

© GREAT SOURCE. COPYING IS PROHIBITED.

BEFORE YOU READ

One tool that can help you read nonfiction is a K-W-L chart.
1. Write anything you think you already know about Amelia Earhart under the "What I Know" (**K**) column.
2. Write what you want to find out under the "What I Want to Know" (**W**) column. You will fill in the **L** column later.
3. Share what you know and want to learn with a partner.

K–W–L CHART

K	W	L
What I Know	What I Want to Know	What I Learned

MY PURPOSE

Who was Amelia Earhart, and what did she do that made her famous?

© GREAT SOURCE. COPYING IS PROHIBITED.

READ

Read this part of a biography about Amelia Earhart.
1. On the first reading, underline facts that are new to you.
2. On the second time through, write comments in the Notes that **make clear** what some of these facts mean to you.

Vanished! The Mysterious Disappearance of Amelia Earhart
by Monica Kulling

Response Notes

Even though Amelia was a <u>skilled</u> pilot, she couldn't get a job flying airplanes. <u>Pilot jobs were scarce</u>, especially for women. Soon her money ran out, and she was forced to sell her plane.

Then, in 1928, Amelia received a phone call. A <u>wealthy</u> woman named Amy Phipps Guest was <u>sponsoring</u> a flight across the Atlantic Ocean. She wanted a woman to be on board. No woman had ever crossed the Atlantic in an airplane.

EXAMPLE:
There were very few female pilots.

skilled—being able to do something well.
scarce—rare; few.
wealthy (wealth•y)—rich.
sponsoring (spon•sor•ing)—helping by giving money or supoort.

© GREAT SOURCE. COPYING IS PROHIBITED.

Amelia jumped at the chance. Even though she would only be a passenger on the flight, it would still be an incredible adventure.

The *Friendship* took off from <u>Trepassey, Newfoundland</u>, on June 17, 1928, with Amelia aboard. After two days of stormy weather—and with less than an hour's worth of gas left—the plane touched down in <u>Burry Port, Wales</u>. Amelia Earhart had become the first woman to cross the Atlantic by air!

Trepassey, Newfoundland (Tre•pas•sey New•found•land)—town in eastern Canada.
Burry Port, Wales (Bur•ry Port, Wales)—town in Wales, a country west of England.

stop and think

Why couldn't Amelia fly the plane?

© GREAT SOURCE. COPYING IS PROHIBITED.

Amelia was famous overnight. Crowds of people gathered to see her. Kings and queens invited her to dine. The President of the United States sent a <u>telegram</u> to <u>congratulate</u> her.

Back home, Amelia was greeted by a huge <u>ticker-tape</u> parade in New York City. But she didn't think she deserved all the attention. She hadn't even flown the plane! Amelia told reporters that she had been nothing more than "a sack of potatoes" on the flight. But she vowed that someday she would fly across the Atlantic Ocean on her own.

telegram (tel•e•gram)—message sent over electrical wires in a code of taps.
congratulate (con•grat•u•late)—show happiness over someone's good fortune.
ticker-tape (tick•er•tape)—paper tape that receives news over a telegraph; small pieces are thrown in parades to honor someone.

© GREAT SOURCE. COPYING IS PROHIBITED.

A publisher named George P. Putnam asked Amelia to write a book about the *Friendship* flight. The book was a huge success. Amelia made enough money to buy a new plane, and before long she was setting records again.

She became the first woman to fly <u>solo</u> across the United States and back. She became the first woman to fly solo across the Pacific Ocean. And, just as she said she would, she became the first woman to fly solo across the Atlantic Ocean.

solo (so•lo)—alone.

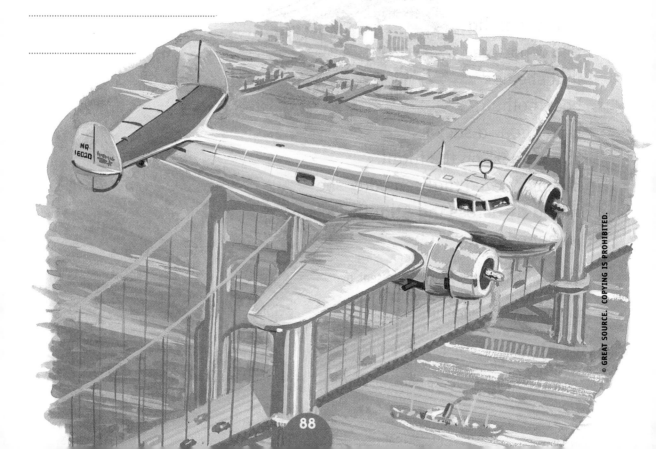

© GREAT SOURCE. COPYING IS PROHIBITED.

By 1936, Amelia was a <u>celebrity</u>. She was also a hero, especially to young women. She spoke at schools across the country, and everywhere she went, she told girls they should not be afraid to follow their dreams. "Women must try to do things, as men have tried," she said. "When they fail, their failure must be but a challenge to others."

celebrity (ce•leb•ri•ty)—famous person.

What are 2 different records that Amelia set?

reread

First fill in the "What I Learned" (**L**) part of the K-W-L chart on page 84. Then read *Vanished!* again. Be sure you have answered each **Stop and Think** question.

© GREAT SOURCE. COPYING IS PROHIBITED.

WORD WORK

You can make long words by combining a word root, such as *tele-*, with small words and other word roots.

tele + gram = *telegram*

1. Complete the word web below by adding *tele-* to words and word roots in the box below.

WORD AND WORD ROOT BOX

graph	phone	scope	vision	photo	type

telegraph

tele-
means to
"operate at a
distance"

2. With a partner, talk about the meanings of these new words. If you need help, use a dictionary.

© GREAT SOURCE. COPYING IS PROHIBITED.

READING REMINDER

Asking questions before and while you read can help you understand the story better.

GET READY TO WRITE

A. ORGANIZE INFORMATION

Get ready to write a news article about Amelia Earhart and the flight of the *Friendship*.

1. A newspaper article should answer the 5 W's—who, what, where, when, and why—and how.

2. In the boxes below, write facts that answer each question.

WHO was sponsoring the flight?

WHAT happened on the flight?

WHERE did it take off and touch down?

WHEN did the flight take place?

HOW did people react to Amelia?

WHY did Amelia want to go on the flight?

© GREAT SOURCE. COPYING IS PROHIBITED.

B. PLAN

A news article has a beginning, a middle, and an end.
Use the storyboards to arrange the details for your news
article about Amelia Earhart.

1. How did the experience start?

Beginning

2. What are 2 or 3 details about what happened?

Middle

3. How did everything turn out?

End

© GREAT SOURCE. COPYING IS PROHIBITED.

WRITE

Write a **news article** about Amelia Earhart's flight on the *Friendship*.
1. Use your notes to describe what happened.
2. Give your article a title.
3. Use the Writers' Checklist to help you edit your article.

Title:

Continue writing on the next page.

© GREAT SOURCE. COPYING IS PROHIBITED.

Continue your article.

WRITERS'
CHECKLIST

Apostrophes

☐ **Did you use apostrophes correctly to show ownership or possession of singular nouns? To show ownership, add an 's to singular nouns.**
EXAMPLES: *Jaimie's sneakers, the man's hat, Tomas's bike*

V. LOOK BACK

What parts of *Vanished!* did you like the most? What parts did you like the least? Write about these parts below.

Think about Your Reading

READERS'
CHECKLIST
Enjoyment

☐ **Was the reading easy to read?**
☐ **Were you able to read it smoothly?**

© GREAT SOURCE. COPYING IS PROHIBITED.

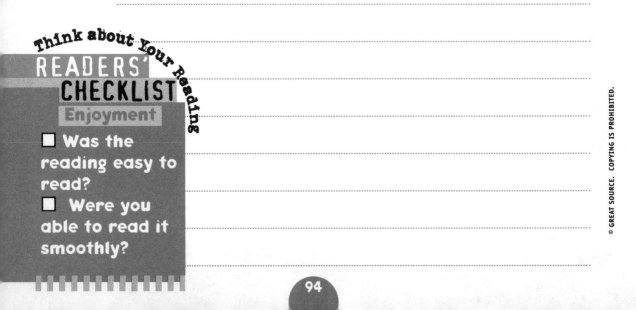

8

Hiroshima

World War II (1939–1945) was one of the most horrible wars in history. In an effort to end the war, the United States dropped an atom bomb on Japan. The bomb destroyed a city called Hiroshima and killed or injured many of the people. After the war, Americans tried to help some of the Japanese who were injured.

© GREAT SOURCE. COPYING IS PROHIBITED.

BEFORE YOU READ

Get a head start on your reading. Preview it. Then predict what *Hiroshima* will be about.

1. Look at the title and the first paragraph of *Hiroshima*.
2. Glance through the rest of the text and read the last paragraph.
3. Then answer the questions below.

What did you learn from the title and first paragraph?

What did you learn from the last paragraph?

What do you think this reading will be about?

MY PURPOSE
What happened to the victims in Hiroshima?

© GREAT SOURCE. COPYING IS PROHIBITED.

READ
Read this part of Laurence Yep's *Hiroshima*.
1. On your first reading, underline parts of the reading that make you ask questions.
2. As you read it a second time, write in the Notes any **questions** that popped into your head.

Hiroshima by Laurence Yep

In 1949, a New York magazine <u>editor</u>, Norman Cousins, visits <u>Hiroshima</u>. He and others become interested in helping the victims of Hiroshima. Though thousands of people need surgery, they decide to start with a small group. <u>The Americans and the Japanese work together.</u> They choose twenty-five women. The American newspapers call the young women "the Hiroshima Maidens."

Many people are <u>determined</u> to help the Maidens. American surgeons will <u>donate</u> their time. American families will provide homes for the Maidens while they receive treatment.

editor (ed•it•or)—person who corrects mistakes on things that have been written.
Hiroshima (Hir•o•shim•a)—city in Japan on which the United States dropped an atom bomb.
determined (de•ter•mined)—stubborn about doing something.
donate (do•nate)—give without receiving anything back.

Response Notes

EXAMPLE:

Didn't America fight the Japanese during World War II?

© GREAT SOURCE. COPYING IS PROHIBITED.

The women leave Hiroshima on an American military transport plane.

DOUBLE-ENTRY JOURNAL

Quote	What You Think This Means
"Remembering the American plane that hurt so many people, they are frightened at first."	

Remembering the American plane that hurt so many people, they are frightened at first. When a soldier tries to serve a cold drink to Sachi, she shakes her head nervously. Another soldier offers her a wet towel to cool herself off. Again she refuses.

Finally, one soldier tries to speak Japanese to Sachi. He knows only a few basic words

© GREAT SOURCE. COPYING IS PROHIBITED.

Response Notes

so he talks in simple sentences like a baby. That makes Sachi smile. She tries to chat with him, but it is hard.

Then Sachi remembers a book each of the women has been given. She takes it out to show him. It is a book of campfire songs. Though she cannot read English, she recognizes the musical notes. She points to the first word. He pronounces it for her. She repeats it until he nods <u>approvingly</u>.

When they have gone through the first page, Sachi slowly tries to sing. The soldier quickly joins in. The other women take out their songbooks. Soon everyone is singing.

approvingly (ap•prov•ing•ly)—done in a way to show that you are happy about what someone else is doing.

© GREAT SOURCE. COPYING IS PROHIBITED.

When the Maidens finally arrive in New York in May 1955, everything is strange and new to them. The food is very different. So are the customs. One woman wants to know where the cowboys are.

Sachi stays with an American family. She is afraid at first. However, she tries to act like a good Japanese daughter.

DOUBLE-ENTRY JOURNAL

Quote	What You Think This Means
"When the Maidens finally arrive in New York in May 1955, everything is strange and new to them."	

GREAT SOURCE. COPYING IS PROHIBITED.

HIROSHIMA (continued)

Her American hosts begin to think of her as one of their own.

Every night she writes down new English words she learns because she wants to talk with her American friends. In turn, she teaches her new friends some of the games she played as a child. It helps <u>occupy</u> her during the recovery from the many operations on her face and arm.

On a television show, one of the <u>crewmen</u> from the <u>Enola Gay</u> sees two of the Maidens. He breaks into tears when he sees what happened to them.

occupy (oc•cu•py)—keep busy.
crewmen (crew•men)—members of the team of pilots who fly the plane.
***Enola Gay* (En•ol•a Gay)**—plane that dropped the atomic bomb on Hiroshima.

© GREAT SOURCE. COPYING IS PROHIBITED.

Over 18 months, 138 free operations are performed on the 25 women. It is a long, painful process. And the surgery is not always successful. One Maiden even dies, but the other women go on bravely with the operations.

reread

Reread *Hiroshima*. Think about what you underlined and the questions you wrote. Be sure you have responded to the quotes in the **Double-entry Journals**.

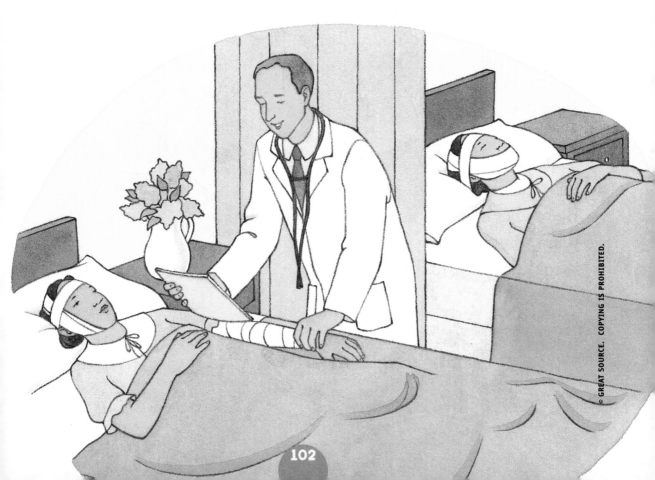

© GREAT SOURCE. COPYING IS PROHIBITED.

WORD WORK

When you see new, long words, they're easy to say if you take off any **prefixes** and **suffixes**. First look for the **base word**, the word part that carries the most meaning. Then try saying the word with the prefix and suffix.

1. Look at the words below.
2. If there's a prefix (*dis-, re-*), put a line through it.
3. If there's a suffix (*-ed, -ment, -ly, -ing, -ful*), put a line through it.
4. Now write the base word.

Long Word	Base Word
treat~~ment~~	treat
remembering	
painful	
recovered	
finally	
frightened	
disappear	
successful	

READING REMINDER

Previewing before you read and asking questions while you read help you get the most out of what you read.

© GREAT SOURCE. COPYING IS PROHIBITED.

III. GET READY TO WRITE

A. CONNECT

One thing *Hiroshima* shows is Sachi's fear and her bravery. Think about a time you were either afraid or brave. What happened? Write 1–2 sentences describing what happened.

B. BRAINSTORM

Brainstorm a list of 3 details that will help you write a journal entry about a time you were afraid or brave. Begin by looking at the model below.

Model:

SUBJECT
The day I got lost in the park

DETAIL #1
wandering off to follow a dog

DETAIL #2
not knowing any of the people or playgrounds

DETAIL #3
finding a police officer and asking for help

SUBJECT

DETAIL #1

DETAIL #2

DETAIL #3

© GREAT SOURCE. COPYING IS PROHIBITED.

IV. WRITE

Now you are ready to write a **journal entry** about a time when you were either afraid or brave.

1. Use details from your brainstorming on page 104.
2. Write in the first person. (Use **I** or **we**.)
3. Use the Writers' Checklist to edit your journal entry.

Date_____

Dear Journal,

....

....

....

....

....

....

....

....

....

....

....

....

....

....

....

....

....

....

....

© GREAT SOURCE. COPYING IS PROHIBITED.

Continue writing on the next page.

Continue your journal entry.

WRITERS' CHECKLIST

End Punctuation

☐ **Did you put a period at the end of sentences that make a statement or give an order?** EXAMPLE: *I ran as fast as a speedboat.*

☐ **Did you put a question mark at the end of sentences that ask a question?** EXAMPLE: *Have you ever been in a helicopter?*

☐ **Did you use an exclamation point at the end of sentences that show strong emotion?** EXAMPLE: *Atlas is a strong kid!*

V. LOOK BACK

In your own words, what would you say *Hiroshima* is about? Write your ideas below.

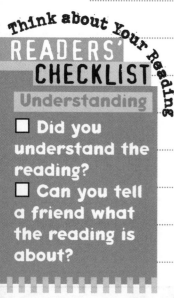

Think about Your Reading

READERS' CHECKLIST

Understanding

☐ **Did you understand the reading?**

☐ **Can you tell a friend what the reading is about?**

© GREAT SOURCE. COPYING IS PROHIBITED.

9

Black Star, Bright Dawn

Every year in Alaska, men and women ride sleds pulled by dogs across the snowy, icy land. They travel hundreds of miles through the freezing cold winds. How do you think you would survive on one of these trips?

© GREAT SOURCE. COPYING IS PROHIBITED.

I. BEFORE YOU READ

When you want to try a new food, you sample it. The same thing works with reading. With a partner, take turns reading the sentences below from *Black Star, Bright Dawn*.

1. Decide which sentence comes first in the story, which comes next, and so on. Number them.
2. Discuss with your partner what you think the sentences mean.
3. Then predict what *Black Star, Bright Dawn* will be about.

☐	"When Black Star was a year old, my father decided that he would never in this world make a good leader."
☐	"On the tenth day of November the sun did not rise."
☐	"Bartok, my father, . . . told me to get the dog sled and harness the dogs."
☐	"After the third day and the streaks of water had not appeared, a blizzard blew from the north and lasted for almost a week."

What do you predict *Black Star, Bright Dawn* will be about?

GREAT SOURCE. COPYING IS PROHIBITED.

MY PURPOSE

Who is Black Star, and what is he like?

READ

Read this part of *Black Star, Bright Dawn*.
1. On your first reading, underline details about Black Star and what is happening.
2. As you read the story again, write in the Notes how you **connect** your own life to parts of the story.

Black Star, Bright Dawn
by Scott O'Dell

On the tenth day of November the sun did not rise. This was the day the sea froze up and there were no more waves. All the birds, except the ravens, flew south and we would not see them again until spring. It was very cold. The air was so still you could hear people talking far away at the end of the village.

My father did not go out on the ice that day. It was thick enough to hold a man's weight, but he waited two days, then three, hoping that leads, streaks of open water, would appear. This is the best time to hunt in the kayak, the little canoe made of deerskin.

After the third day and the streaks of open water had not appeared, a blizzard blew from the north and lasted for almost a week.

ravens (ra•vens)—black birds, like crows.
kayak (kay•ak)—Eskimo canoe made from skins.
blizzard (bliz•zard)—blinding snowstorm.

Response Notes

EXAMPLE:
I watch the geese fly south through our town.

© GREAT SOURCE. COPYING IS PROHIBITED.

It brought floating ice down from the Bering Sea, and the <u>polar</u> ice pounded against the ice along the shore.

DOUBLE-ENTRY JOURNAL

Quote	What You Think This Means
"My father did not go out on the ice that day. It was thick enough to hold a man's weight, but he waited two days, then three. . . ."	

Bartok, my father, decided not to wait for the leads to open. He told me to get the dog sled and <u>harness</u> the dogs. He would hunt without a kayak.

"We'll hunt bearded seals on the ice," he said.

Bearded seals are heavy. They can weigh six hundred pounds. I

polar (po•lar)—something from the north or south poles.
harness (har•ness)—hook an animal to something to be pulled.

© GREAT SOURCE. COPYING IS PROHIBITED.

BLACK STAR, BRIGHT DAWN (continued)

harnessed our seven dogs to the sled and chose Black Star to lead the team. Bartok did not like him. When Black Star was a year old, my father decided that he would never in this world make a good leader.

"He's <u>stubborn</u>," my father said. "You tell him something and he does something else."

"He's smart," I said, remembering the winter when we were coming home and, just on the other side of Salmon Creek, Black Star pulled up and wouldn't move. My father took the whip to him and still he wouldn't move. Then my father walked out on the frozen creek and fell through the ice up to his neck. I remembered this time but said nothing about it. "Black Star knows a lot," I said.

"Of the wrong things," Bartok said. "He's got too much wolf in him. His father came from Baffin Bay and had a lot of wolf blood. They <u>bred</u> him to a Siberian husky. So he's mostly wolf."

stubborn (stub•born)—not changing the mind easily.
bred—had him have babies with.

© GREAT SOURCE. COPYING IS PROHIBITED.

Quote	What You Think This Means
" 'Black Star knows a lot,' I said. 'Of the wrong things,' Bartok said. 'He's got too much wolf in him.' "	

Response Notes

BLACK STAR, BRIGHT DAWN (continued)

I liked Black Star. I had liked him since he was a month old. There were seven in the litter and he was the most playful of them all. He bounced around and took nothing from his brothers and sisters, giving two bites for every one he got.

He was of the purest white, with a black star on his forehead and black slashes under big eyes. But of everything, it was his eyes themselves that <u>captured</u> me.

captured (cap•tured)—held; attracted.

reread

Reread *Black Star, Bright Dawn*. Think about what Black Star is like. On this reading, be sure you have responded to each quote in the **Double-entry Journals**.

© GREAT SOURCE. COPYING IS PROHIBITED.

WORD WORK

Sometimes when you add a **suffix** to a word, no change is needed. You simply add the suffix. Other times, you need to drop a *final e* before adding a suffix.

EXAMPLE:

No change:
wait + ing = *waiting*

Drop *final e:*
ice + ing = *icing*

Use the examples above to help you add the suffixes to the words below.

1. appear + ed

2. hope + ing

3. open + ing

4. come + ing

5. pound + ed

6. decide + ed

7. remember + ing

8. capture + ed

© GREAT SOURCE. COPYING IS PROHIBITED.

READING REMINDER

Making predictions about what will happen can help you get more from your reading.

III. GET READY TO WRITE

A. BRAINSTORM

Black Star, Bright Dawn is set in winter. Think about things you like about winter.

1. Brainstorm ideas about your favorite wintertime sights, sounds, smells, tastes, and activities.
2. Try to write 1–2 ideas in each box. One has been done for you.

SIGHTS

SOUNDS

a crackling fire

SMELLS

TASTES

What I Like About Winter

ACTIVITIES

© GREAT SOURCE. COPYING IS PROHIBITED.

B. LOOK AT A MODEL

Study the parts of a model letter. Then use the model to help you write a letter that explains what you like about winter.

1. date → November 22, 2000

Dear Ricky, ← **2. greeting**

3. body → I'm coming to New Hampshire to see you later this month. Please think of some cool stuff we can do. I can't wait to go skiing and skating. Let's have hot chocolate when we sit by the crackling fire.

4. closing → Your friend,

5. signature → Luis

© GREAT SOURCE. COPYING IS PROHIBITED.

IV. WRITE

Write a **letter** to a friend. Explain what you like about winter.
1. Reread your brainstorming ideas on page 114.
2. Write a separate sentence for each detail.
3. End with a sentence that tells your own feelings about winter.
4. Use the Writers' Checklist to edit your letter.

Continue writing on the next page.

© GREAT SOURCE. COPYING IS PROHIBITED.

© GREAT SOURCE. COPYING IS PROHIBITED.

WRITERS' CHECKLIST

Run-on Sentences

☐ **Did you avoid run-on sentences?** EXAMPLE: *Snow covers the trees it looks peaceful. (run-on)*

Here are two easy ways to fix a run-on sentence:

1. Break it apart into two sentences.

EXAMPLE: *Snow covers the trees. It looks peaceful.*

2. Put in a comma and a conjunction (and, or, but, so) to make a compound sentence.

EXAMPLE: *Snow covers the trees, and it looks peaceful.*

V. LOOK BACK

What did *Black Star, Bright Dawn* make you think about?
Write your answer below.

....

....

....

....

....

Think about Your Reading

READERS' CHECKLIST

Meaning

- ☐ Did you learn something from the reading?
- ☐ Did you have a strong feeling about one part of the reading?

....

....

....

....

....

© GREAT SOURCE. COPYING IS PROHIBITED.

10

Animal Fact/ Animal Fable

Owls are very wise. Turkeys are dumb. Mules are stubborn. Have you ever heard that? Sometimes it is hard to figure out what is true in a story and what is not true. Can you think of other stories you have heard about animals?

GREAT SOURCE. COPYING IS PROHIBITED.

I.
BEFORE YOU READ
Preview *Animal Fact/Animal Fable*.
1. Look at the pictures.
2. Read the first sentence of each paragraph.
3. Then answer these questions.

In your own words, what does the word <u>fact</u> mean?

_____

_____

_____

_____

_____

In your own words, what does the word <u>fable</u> mean?

_____

_____

_____

_____

_____

MY
PURPOSE
What are some facts and fables about animals?

©GREAT SOURCE. COPYING IS PROHIBITED.

READ

Read this part of *Animal Fact/Animal Fable*.
1. As you read it the first time, underline the details about animals that are facts.
2. As you read it a second time, write comments in the Notes that **make clear** what you think of some of these animal facts.

Animal Fact/Animal Fable
by Seymour Simon

<u>FABLE</u> Since early times, people have said that cats have nine lives. In Egypt, a long time ago, cats were even thought to be gods. <u>Cats are so quick and clever</u> that sometimes it may seem as if the fable is fact. But cats, like all animals, have only one life to lose. Many animals can hurt themselves if they fall from a height. But cats are so <u>nimble</u> that they usually land on their feet and walk away. Cats jump

Response Notes

EXAMPLE:
I didn't know cats were smart!

FABLE (fa•ble)—story that is exaggerated or not true.
nimble (nim•ble)—quick and light in movement.

© GREAT SOURCE. COPYING IS PROHIBITED.

and move about so easily that it seems as if they are never hurt. Of course, that's not so. Cats do get hurt. . . .

STOP AND RETELL stop and retell STOP AND RETELL

What are 2 fables about cats?

1.

2.

STOP AND RETELL STOP AND RETELL STOP AND RETELL

FACT Goats will eat almost anything they can find. They even seem to eat tin cans. But they are not really eating the metal can; they are chewing the label to get at the glue underneath.

Though goats eat string and paper, they would rather eat fruit, vegetables, grass, and leaves of plants. They are not quite the "garbage cans" some people think they are.

© GREAT SOURCE. COPYING IS PROHIBITED.

STOP AND RETELL stop and retell STOP AND RETELL

What are 2 facts about goats?

1.

2.

STOP AND RETELL STOP AND RETELL STOP AND RETELL

ANIMAL FACT/ANIMAL FABLE (continued)

Response Notes

FABLE A snake uses its tongue to smell rather than to bite. Snakes have <u>forked</u> tongues that <u>flick</u> in and out. The forked tongue may look sharp, but the snake can't really bite anything with it. Its tongue is much too soft to cause an <u>injury</u>.

A snake's tongue picks up the smell of animals in the air. The tongue then carries the smell back into the snake's mouth. This helps the snake to track its <u>prey</u>.

forked—divided.
flick—move in a light, quick way.
injury (in•jur•y)—something that is hurt on a body.
prey—something hunted.

© GREAT SOURCE. COPYING IS PROHIBITED.

What are 2 facts about snakes?

1.

2.

Response Notes

ANIMAL FACT/ANIMAL FABLE (continued)

FACT It is a fact that rats will try to jump overboard if a ship is sinking. But that is true of any animal that can swim, and even some that can't. Rats sometimes <u>desert</u> a ship even if it isn't sinking. In the days of sailing ships, it was a common sight to see packs of rats jumping overboard.

desert (des•ert)—leave.

©GREAT SOURCE. COPYING IS PROHIBITED.

Sailing ships were slow. They stayed at sea for many months. By the time a ship returned to port, there was little food left for the rats. When the ship came close to shore, the hungry rats would dive overboard and swim to land to find food.

reread

Reread *Animal Fact/Animal Fable*. As you do, be sure you have answered each of the **Stop and Retell** questions.

© GREAT SOURCE. COPYING IS PROHIBITED.

WORD WORK

You should know the 1-1-1 rule. If a 1-syllable word ends in 1 consonant and there is 1 vowel in front of that consonant, double the final consonant when you add a **suffix** that starts with a vowel.

1-syllable word (*sit*) ending in 1 consonant (*t*), with 1 vowel in front of that consonant (*i*):

sit + ing = *sitting*

But the rule does not work for words that end in *x*:

box + ing = *boxing*

1. Add the suffixes to the 1-syllable words below. Follow the rule and double the final consonant.
2. One has been done for you.

flag + ing ⟶ flagging

dim + er ⟶

ship + ed ⟶

swim + er ⟶

get + ing ⟶

tip + ing ⟶

step + ed ⟶

© GREAT SOURCE. COPYING IS PROHIBITED.

READING REMINDER

Previewing helps you start to understand ideas and think about a reading so that you can remember more.

III. GET READY TO WRITE

A. CHOOSE A TOPIC

Expository writing gives information about a topic. Choose a topic to write an expository paragraph about.

1. Jot down the names of 2 animals and 2 sports.
2. Then circle the one you know the most about.
3. Write some of the facts you know about the topic you circled.

Animals
1.
2.
Sports
1.
2.

Facts about my topic

B. WRITE A TOPIC SENTENCE

Now write a topic sentence for a paragraph telling about the topic you chose. A topic sentence tells what the paragraph is going to be about. Use this formula.

(a specific topic) + (a specific feeling about the topic) = a good topic sentence

Example: (Soccer) + (It is a very challenging sport) = Soccer is a very challenging sport.

My topic sentence:

© GREAT SOURCE. COPYING IS PROHIBITED.

C. GATHER DETAILS

The body of a paragraph gives details to support the topic sentence. Study the example paragraph below.
1. Write your topic sentence in the space below.
2. Then list 3 details that support your topic sentence.
3. Write a closing sentence that restates your topic sentence.

Example

TOPIC SENTENCE: Soccer is a very challenging sport.

Detail #1: The players run almost the whole game.

Detail #2: Players even use their heads to make shots.

Detail #3: It is difficult to score goals.

CLOSING SENTENCE: Soccer is an incredibly hard sport to play.

TOPIC SENTENCE:

Detail #1:

Detail #2:

Detail #3:

CLOSING SENTENCE:

© GREAT SOURCE. COPYING IS PROHIBITED.

IV. WRITE

Write an **expository paragraph** about the animal or sport you chose. Give it a title.

1. Begin with your topic sentence.
2. Include 3 details. Each detail should be its own sentence.
3. End with a closing sentence.
4. Use the Writers' Checklist to edit your paragraph.

Title:

© GREAT SOURCE. COPYING IS PROHIBITED.

Continue writing on the next page.

Continue your paragraph.

....

....

....

....

....

....

....

....

WRITERS' CHECKLIST

Fragments

☐ **Did you avoid writing sentence fragments?**
Remember that a complete sentence needs a subject and a verb and should make sense by itself.
EXAMPLE: *The elephant under the tree.*
(fragment)
The elephant <u>stood</u> *under the tree.*
(complete sentence)

LOOK BACK

What would you tell a friend about *Animal Fact/Animal Fable*?
Write about 2–3 of these things below.

Think about Your Reading

READERS' CHECKLIST

Understanding

☐ **Did you understand the reading?**
☐ **Can you tell a friend what the reading is about?**

© GREAT SOURCE. COPYING IS PROHIBITED.

11

Very Last First Time

What sort of things show that you are growing up? Do you have a job? Are you getting stronger? In cultures around the world, children often must perform a special task to show that they are ready to be adults.

© GREAT SOURCE. IS PROHIBITED.

I. BEFORE YOU READ

Get ready to read by getting a feeling for the subject.
1. Read the sentences below.
2. With your reading partner, read the title and the first 3 paragraphs of *Very Last First Time*.
3. Then circle what you think will and won't happen and make a prediction.
4. Share and discuss your answers with your reading partner.

DEFINITELY WON'T HAPPEN			DEFINITELY WILL HAPPEN		
1	2	3	4	5	Eva will be too scared to go on the walk by herself.
1	2	3	4	5	Something good will happen to Eva at the bottom of the sea.
1	2	3	4	5	There will be no mussels at the bottom of the sea.
1	2	3	4	5	Eva will be alone for the first time.

MY PREDICTION: I think this story will be about

....

....

....

....

....

....

....

MY PURPOSE
What will happen to Eva?

© GREAT SOURCE. COPYING IS PROHIBITED.

READ

Read this part of *Very Last First Time*.

1. On your first reading, underline parts that help you see a picture of Eva and the story in your mind.

2. As you read the story a second time, **draw** in the Notes what you see.

Very Last First Time
by Jan Andrews

Response Notes

Eva Padlyat lived in a village on Ungava Bay in northern Canada. She was <u>Inuit</u>, and ever since she could remember she had walked with her mother on the bottom of the sea. It was something the people of her village did in winter when they wanted <u>mussels</u> to eat.

Today, something very special was going to happen. Today, for the very first time in her life, Eva would walk on the bottom of the sea alone.

Eva got ready. Standing in their small, warm kitchen, Eva looked at her mother and smiled.

"Shall we go now?"

"I think we'd better."

EXAMPLE:

Inuit (In•u•it)—Eskimo tribe in northern Canada.
mussels (mus•sels)—sea creatures with a shell.

© GREAT SOURCE. COPYING IS PROHIBITED.

133

"We'll start out together, won't we?"

Eva's mother nodded. Pulling up their warm hoods, they went out.

Eva and her mother walked carefully over the bumps and <u>ridges</u> of the frozen sea. Soon they found a spot where the ice was cracked and broken.

"This is the right place," Eva said.

ridges (rid•ges)— slopes; bumps.

stop and think

Why is Eva going to walk on the bottom of the sea?

© GREAT SOURCE. COPYING IS PROHIBITED.

VERY LAST FIRST TIME (continued)

After shoveling away a pile of snow, she reached for the <u>ice-chisel</u>. She worked it under an ice hump and, heaving and pushing with her mother's help, made a hole.

Eva <u>peered</u> down into the hole and felt the dampness of the air below. She breathed deep to catch the salt sea smell.

"Good luck," Eva's mother said.

Eva grinned. "Good luck yourself."

Her eyes lit up with excitement and she threw her mussel pan into the hole. Then she lowered herself slowly into the darkness, feeling with her feet until they touched a rock and she could let go of the ice above.

In a minute, she was standing on the <u>seabed</u>.

Above her, in the ice hole, the wind whistled. Eva struck a match and lit a candle. The gold-bright flame shone and <u>glistened</u> on the wet stones and pools at her feet.

ice-chisel (ice chis•el)—hammer that breaks away ice.
peered—looked.
seabed (sea•bed)—bottom of the sea.
glistened (glis•tened)—sparkled; glittered.

© GREAT SOURCE. COPYING IS PROHIBITED.

What is Eva doing in the ice hole?

Response Notes

VERY LAST FIRST TIME (continued)

She held her candle and saw strange shadow shapes around her. The shadows formed a wolf, a bear, a seal sea-monster. Eva watched them, then she remembered.

"I'd better get to work," she said.

Lighting three more candles, she carefully <u>wedged</u> them between stones so she could see to collect mussels. Using her knife as a <u>lever</u>, she <u>tugged</u> and <u>pried</u> and scraped to pull the mussels off the rocks. She was in luck. There were strings of

wedged—pushed something in tightly between two objects so it doesn't move.
lever (lev•er)—something like a bar that lifts a weight.
tugged—pulled.
pried—forced open with a lever.

© GREAT SOURCE. COPYING IS PROHIBITED.

136

VERY LAST FIRST TIME (continued)

blue-black mussel shells whichever
way she turned.

Alone—for the first time.

Eva was so happy she started
to sing.

reread

Reread *Very Last First Time*. On this reading, think about
what Eva does. Be sure you've answered all of the **Stop and
Think** questions.

©GREAT SOURCE. COPYING IS PROHIBITED.

WORD WORK

There are different rules to follow when adding **suffixes** to words. Here are 3 of the most common:

Drop *final e*: bake + ing = *baking*
Double final consonant: tap + ed = *tapped*
No change: correct + ed = *corrected*

1. Add suffixes to each word below.
2. Use the rules to help you.

Word	+	Suffix	=	New Word
1. wedge	+	ed	=	
2. shadow	+	ing	=	
3. drop	+	ed	=	
4. walk	+	ing	=	
5. shape	+	ing	=	
6. tug	+	ed	=	

READING REMINDER

Predicting before you read and asking questions while you read can help you understand the story better.

GREAT SOURCE. COPYING IS PROHIBITED.

III. GET READY TO WRITE

A. ORGANIZE WHAT YOU KNOW

Reflect on what happens to Eva.

1. Fill in the story chart with details from the story.

2. Look back at the story to help you remember.

Very Last First Time

1 Setting
Where and when does the story take place?

2 Main Characters
Who are the main characters?

3 Problem
What problem does Eva face?

4 Solution
How is the problem solved?

GREAT SOURCE. COPYING IS PROHIBITED.

B. PLAN

Very Last First Time is about a girl who must do a job that shows that she is growing up. Get ready to write a paragraph about something that you have done or will do that shows you are growing up.

1. Use the storyboards below to tell your story.

2. Complete the sentences below.

#1

When I was/am _____ years old

#2

Then

#3

After that

#4

Finally

#5

I felt/will feel

GREAT SOURCE. COPYING IS PROHIBITED.

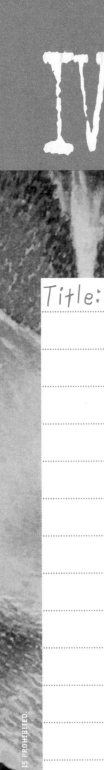

IV. WRITE

Write a **narrative paragraph** (a paragraph that tells a story) about an experience that shows you are growing up.

1. Begin with a topic sentence about what you have done or will do.
2. Give at least 2 different details. Use your storyboards from page 140. Start a new sentence for each detail.
3. Write a closing sentence that tells how you feel about growing up.
4. Use the Writers' Checklist to edit your paragraph.

Title:

GREAT SOURCE. COPYING IS PROHIBITED.

Continue writing on the next page.

Continue your paragraph.

....

....

....

....

....

....

....

....

....

WRITERS' CHECKLIST

Capitalization

☐ **Did you capitalize the names of particular persons, places, and things?**
EXAMPLE: *My sister, Mia, works at the Woodland Library.*

☐ **Did you capitalize the pronoun *I*?**
EXAMPLE: *Marcus and I took the mail in for the neighbors.*

V. LOOK BACK

Was *Very Last First Time* easy to read? Why or why not? Write your reasons below.

....

....

....

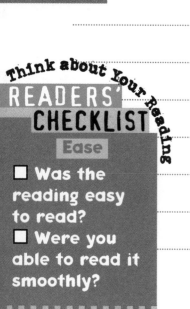

Think about Your Reading

READERS' CHECKLIST

Ease

☐ **Was the reading easy to read?**
☐ **Were you able to read it smoothly?**

© GREAT SOURCE. COPYING IS PROHIBITED.

12

If You Lived with the Sioux Indians

What would it be like to have to hunt for your food? Many Native-American tribes hunted buffalo. They used the buffalo for food, clothing, weapons, and shelter. The hunt was an important part of their lives.

GREAT SOURCE. COPYING IS PROHIBITED.

I. BEFORE YOU READ

Using a K-W-L chart can help you keep track of what you know and what you want to learn. Fill in the chart below.

1. Write all you think you already know about how Native Americans hunted for food long ago under the **K.**
2. Write what you want to know under the **W.** You will fill in the **L** column later.
3. Share what you know and what you want to learn with a partner.

K-W-L CHART

K	W	L
What I Know	What I Want to Know	What I Learned

GREAT SOURCE. COPYING IS PROHIBITED.

MY PURPOSE

How did Native Americans hunt for food?

READ

Read this part of *If You Lived with the Sioux Indians*.

1. When you first read it, underline parts that explain how Native Americans hunted long ago.
2. When you read it a second time, write the **questions** that pop into your mind in the Notes.
3. When you find answers to your questions, jot these in the Notes too.

If You Lived with the Sioux Indians
by Ann McGovern

How did the <u>Sioux</u> *hunt the buffalo?*

Each hunt was carefully planned at a <u>council</u> meeting. The chiefs chose the leaders of the hunt. <u>They chose men who would keep</u> order. They chose scouts to ride out and find the huge <u>herd</u> of buffalo. Some men were chosen to do the hunting for other members of the tribe—for those who were too old or too sick to hunt for themselves.

Sioux—Native-American tribe.
council (coun•cil)—group of people who get together to discuss or advise.
herd—group of animals.

Response Notes

EXAMPLE:

What happened if the chiefs couldn't agree?

© GREAT SOURCE. COPYING IS PROHIBITED.

It might take the <u>scouts</u> weeks before they found buffalo. Meanwhile, everyone in camp was busy. It was a time for playing games, dancing, and singing. It was a time for worshipping. It was a time for visiting friendly tribes nearby and trading with them.

When the scouts returned with the news that a buffalo herd was found, the camp moved. They wanted to be as close to the buffalo herd as possible.

On the day of the hunt, every hunter <u>mounted</u> his horse.

scouts—lookouts who go ahead to see what might be there.
mounted (mount•ed)—got up on top of something, like an animal.

© GREAT SOURCE. COPYING IS PROHIBITED.

SIOUX INDIANS (continued)

At a <u>signal</u> from the chief, the men <u>charged</u>. The buffalo began to run, making clouds of dust. The hunters aimed their arrows at the buffalo's heart. The buffalo ran so fast the hunters had time to shoot only three arrows before the stop-shooting signal was given. A buffalo hunt took about ten minutes.

No one was allowed to kill more buffalo than the tribe could use.

signal (sig•nal)—sign that tells someone something.
charged—moved forward quickly.

STOP AND RETELL stop and retell STOP AND RETELL

What 3 things have you learned about how the Sioux hunt so far?

1.

2.

3.

STOP AND RETELL STOP AND RETELL STOP AND RETELL

© GREAT SOURCE. COPYING IS PROHIBITED.

Did boys take part in the hunt?

Hunting buffalo was dangerous. A boy might get knocked over by a charging buffalo. A horse might fall and throw a boy right into the middle of the underlined stampeding buffalo.

It was too dangerous for boys to ride with the hunters. But they were allowed to tag along far behind the hunters. The boys rode their own colts. With their bows and arrows, they shot the young buffalo calves that followed the herd.

stampeding (stam•**ped**•ing)—running in a scared way.

STOP AND RETELL **stop** and **retell** **STOP AND RETELL**

Why was a buffalo hunt dangerous?

© GREAT SOURCE. COPYING IS PROHIBITED.

STOP AND RETELL STOP AND RETELL STOP AND RETELL

SIOUX INDIANS (continued)

Boys were expected to hunt their first buffalo calf before they were ten years old.

What happened after the hunt?

The women followed the hunters with their pack horses. The men helped the women <u>skin</u> the buffalo, cut up the meat, and load it on the horses.

They all rode back to the camp and the fun and <u>feasting</u> began.

If a boy had hunted his first buffalo, his family might give him a feast—but he would not be allowed to eat any of the buffalo

skin—remove skin from an animal.
feasting (feast•ing)—eating and celebrating.

© GREAT SOURCE. COPYING IS PROHIBITED.

meat himself! That was to teach him it was wrong to want things for himself alone.

Songs were made up and sung in his honor. And his family might hold a *give-away*. A give-away was like a birthday party—but the gifts were given to the guests!

After the give-away, the boy's family wouldn't have much left. They knew that sooner or later the guests would bring gifts back to them. But what about the things they needed right away? The family had to get busy and make them.

STOP AND RETELL stop and retell STOP AND RETELL

How did a family celebrate a boy's first buffalo?

STOP AND RETELL STOP AND RETELL STOP AND RETELL

reread

Reread *If You Lived with the Sioux Indians.* Before you do, be sure to complete the **L** part of the chart on page 144. Then be sure you have answered all of the **Stop and Retell** questions.

© GREAT SOURCE. COPYING IS PROHIBITED.

WORD WORK

Many words you read sound the same, but they have a different spelling: *they're, their, there; bare, bear.*

We call these words **homophones**. Below are some homophones from *If You Lived with the Sioux Indians*. Read the homophones and examples below.

two—a number that comes after one
Example: He has two kittens.

to—toward
Example: Please walk to me.

too—also or very
Examples: You can come too.
    Don't be too late.

here—pointing out a place
Example: The bicycle is here.

hear—to listen to
Example: I can hear that man sing.

Now put the correct homophone in each sentence below.

1. Did you _____ the band last night?

2. Jamal has _____ sisters and a brother.

3. At dinner I ate _____ much cake.

4. The team ran _____ the park and by the lake.

5. We _____ that dog bark every night.

6. You can park your car _____ .

READING REMINDER

Thinking about what you already know and questioning what you want to learn are important. They help give you direction as you read.

© GREAT SOURCE. COPYING IS PROHIBITED.

III. GET READY TO WRITE

A. COMPARE AND CONTRAST

Get ready to write a paragraph comparing your family's life to that of a Sioux Indian family from long ago.

1. Write words that describe Sioux families on the left.
2. Write words describing your family's life on the right.
3. Put things you have in common in the middle.

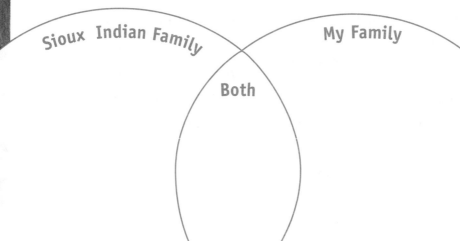

Sioux Indian Family   My Family

Both

B. PLAN YOUR PARAGRAPH

Write 3 details you want to include in your paragraph comparing your family's life to a Sioux Indian family's life.

1. ....

2. ....

3. ....

GREAT SOURCE. COPYING IS PROHIBITED.

WRITE

Write a **compare and contrast paragraph** about your family's life and the life of a Sioux Indian family from long ago.

1. Begin with a topic sentence that tells what the paragraph will be about.

2. In the body of the paragraph, give 3 supporting details. Start a new sentence for each detail.

3. Use the Writers' Checklist to help you edit.

Title:

Continue writing on the next page.

© GREAT SOURCE. COPYING IS PROHIBITED.

Continue your paragraph.

....

....

....

....

....

....

WRITERS' CHECKLIST

Homophones

☐ **Did you correctly use the words *to*, *two*, and *too*?**
EXAMPLES: *We went to the skating rink. I fell two times. My brother fell, too.*
☐ **Did you correctly use the words *hear* and *here*?** EXAMPLES: *I hear them singing. Come over here for dinner.*

V. LOOK BACK

What parts did you like best about *If You Lived with the Sioux Indians*? Write your answer below.

....

....

....

....

....

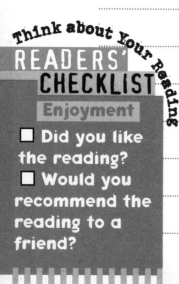

Think about Your Reading

READERS' CHECKLIST

Enjoyment

☐ **Did you like the reading?**
☐ **Would you recommend the reading to a friend?**

© GREAT SOURCE. COPYING IS PROHIBITED.

13

John Henry

Can a person be stronger than a machine? Can a person work twice as fast as a machine? Can someone blast through a mountain? According to the stories told, a man named John Henry could.

GREAT SOURCE. COPYING IS PROHIBITED.

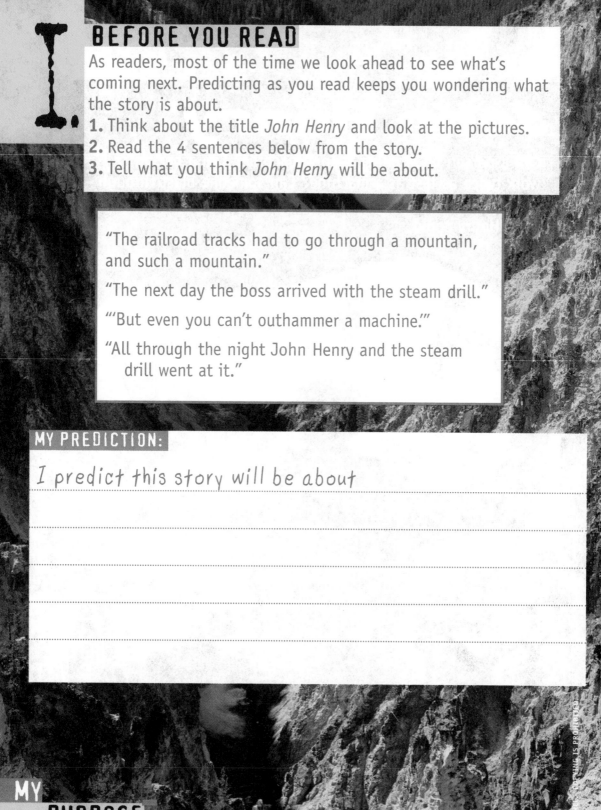

BEFORE YOU READ

As readers, most of the time we look ahead to see what's coming next. Predicting as you read keeps you wondering what the story is about.

1. Think about the title *John Henry* and look at the pictures.
2. Read the 4 sentences below from the story.
3. Tell what you think *John Henry* will be about.

"The railroad tracks had to go through a mountain, and such a mountain."

"The next day the boss arrived with the steam drill."

"'But even you can't outhammer a machine.'"

"All through the night John Henry and the steam drill went at it."

MY PREDICTION:

I predict this story will be about

MY PURPOSE

What did John Henry do?

© GREAT SOURCE. COPYING IS PROHIBITED.

II. READ

Read this part of the story *John Henry*.
1. On your first reading, underline details about what John Henry does that **connect** to your feelings and experiences.
2. As you read it again, jot down your thoughts in the Notes.

John Henry by Julius Lester

John Henry went on his way. He had heard that <u>any man good with a hammer could find work building the Chesapeake and Ohio Railroad</u> through West Virginia. That was where he had been going when he stopped to build the road.

The next day John Henry arrived at the railroad. However, work had stopped. The railroad tracks had to go through a mountain, and such a mountain. Next to it even John Henry felt small.

But a worker told John Henry about a new machine they were going to use to <u>tunnel</u> through the mountain. It was called a steam drill. "It can hammer faster and harder than ten men and it never has to stop and rest."

tunnel (tun•nel)—make a hole that goes all the way through something underground or underwater.

Response Notes

EXAMPLE:

He must have been really strong. I wouldn't like that kind of work.

© GREAT SOURCE. COPYING IS PROHIBITED.

157

!!*!*!* stop and organize !*!*!*!*!*

Use this organizer to show what you know so far.

Who is the main character?	Where does the story take place?

STOP AND ORGANIZE STOP AND ORGANIZE

Response Notes

JOHN HENRY (continued)

The next day the boss arrived with the steam drill. John Henry said to him, "Let's have a contest. Your steam drill against me and my hammers."

The man laughed. "I've heard you're the best there ever was, John Henry. But even you can't outhammer a machine."

"Let's find out," John Henry answered.

GREAT SOURCE. COPYING IS PROHIBITED.

JOHN HENRY (continued)

Boss shrugged. "Don't make me no never mind. You start on the other side of the mountain. I'll start the steam drill over here. Whoever gets to the middle first is the winner". . . .

!!* *!*! stop and organize *!*!*!*!*

What is the problem in this story?

STOP AND ORGANIZE STOP AND ORGANIZE

All through the night John Henry and the steam drill went at it. In the light from the <u>tongues</u> of fire shooting out of the tunnel from John Henry's hammer <u>blows</u>, folks could see the rainbow wrapped around the mountain like a <u>shawl</u>.

tongues—flames.
blows—hard hits.
shawl—long piece of cloth worn as a covering for the head, neck, and shoulders.

GREAT SOURCE. COPYING IS PROHIBITED.

The sun came up extra early the next morning to see who was winning. Just as it did, John Henry broke through and met the steam drill. The boss of the steam drill was <u>flabbergasted.</u> John Henry had come a mile and a quarter. The steam drill had only come a quarter.

Folks were cheering and yelling, "John Henry! John Henry!"

flabbergasted (**flab**•ber•gast•ed)—shocked.

stop and organize

What happens at the end? How is the problem solved?

reread

Reread *John Henry*. Think about your reactions to what John Henry did. As you read, be sure you have completed all of the **Stop and Organize** questions.

© GREAT SOURCE. COPYING IS PROHIBITED.

WORD WORK

You can put 2 small words together to form a **compound word**:

rail + road = *railroad*   out + hammer = *outhammer*

1. Make 6 compound words.
2. Begin each with a different word from Column 1. Add to it a word from Column 2.

Column 1	Column 2
hill	ring
home	board
camp	top
chalk	sick
head	fire
ear	ache

1. ....
2. ....
3. ....
4. ....
5. ....
6. ....

GREAT SOURCE. COPYING IS PROHIBITED.

READING REMINDER

Making personal connections to what you're reading helps you stay interested in what's being described.

A. REFLECT ON PLOT

Plot is the events or action in a story. It is all of the things that happen in a story. A good plot has a beginning, a middle, and an end.

1. Work on these 3 plot questions with your reading partner.

2. Write your answers below.

1. What happens at the beginning of John Henry?

2. What happens in the middle of John Henry?

3. What happens at the end of John Henry?

© GREAT SOURCE. COPYING IS PROHIBITED.

B. CREATE AN ENDING

Get ready to write a new ending for *John Henry*.

1. Complete the storyboard for a possible new ending. Begin right after the contest between John Henry and Boss begins.
2. Tell 3 things that happen.

> John Henry begins hammering, and Boss starts the steam drill.

1. What John Henry does next	2. What Boss does	3. How the story ends

GREAT SOURCE. COPYING IS PROHIBITED.

WRITE

Write a new **story ending** for *John Henry*.
1. Use your notes from the storyboard on page 163.
2. Use the Writers' Checklist to edit your ending.

My Ending to John Henry

Continue writing on the next page.

© GREAT SOURCE. COPYING IS PROHIBITED.

Continue your story ending.

WRITERS' CHECKLIST

Capitalization

☐ Did you capitalize titles? EXAMPLES: **M**r. John Henry, **D**r. Smith

☐ Did you capitalize the names of particular geographical features? EXAMPLES: **A**ppalachian **M**ountains, **A**tlantic **O**cean, **L**ake **M**ichigan

© GREAT SOURCE. COPYING IS PROHIBITED.

V. LOOK BACK

What parts of *John Henry* were easy to read? What parts were hard to read? Write your thoughts below.

....

....

....

....

....

....

....

....

....

....

....

Think about Your Reading

READERS' CHECKLIST

Ease

☐ Was the reading easy to read?

☐ Were you able to read it smoothly?

© GREAT SOURCE. COPYING IS PROHIBITED.

14

On the Banks of Plum Creek

Have you ever waited for a letter or a package to come from someone special? Did you check the mailbox again and again? Did you imagine that the letter was lost or that something terrible happened to the sender? Sometimes, waiting is really hard.

© GREAT SOURCE. COPYING IS PROHIBITED.

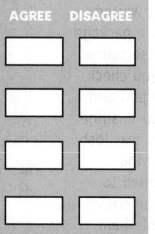

I. BEFORE YOU READ

Start to think about a subject before you begin reading about it.

1. Read the statements below. If you agree, check the AGREE box. If you disagree, check the DISAGREE box.
2. Share your ideas with your reading partner.
3. Finally, read the first paragraph of the selection and make a prediction.

AGREE	DISAGREE	
☐	☐	Thinking about someone you miss can make you sad.
☐	☐	An adult should not let a child know how he or she is feeling.
☐	☐	Time goes more quickly when you don't watch the clock.
☐	☐	Having a good imagination helps you through hard times.

MY PREDICTION: *I think this story will be about*

© GREAT SOURCE. COPYING IS PROHIBITED.

MY PURPOSE

Who is waiting, and what is she waiting for?

READ

Read this part of *On the Banks of Plum Creek*.
1. On your first reading, underline parts of the story that help you find out whom Laura is waiting for and why.
2. On your next reading, **draw** sketches in the Notes of what you see as you read.

On the Banks of Plum Creek
by Laura Ingalls Wilder

All day long Laura missed Pa, and at night when the wind blew <u>lonesomely</u> over the dark land, she felt <u>hollow</u> and <u>aching</u>.

At first she talked about him; she wondered how far he had walked that day; she hoped his old, <u>patched</u> boots were lasting; <u>she wondered where he was camping that night.</u> Later she did not speak about him to Ma. Ma was thinking about him all the time and she did not like to talk about it. She did not like even to count the days till Saturday.

lonesomely (lone•some•ly)—sadly; in a lonely way.
hollow (hol•low)—empty.
aching (ach•ing)—hurting in a dull, steady way.
patched—fixed with material sewn over holes.

Response Notes

EXAMPLE:

© GREAT SOURCE. COPYING IS PROHIBITED.

Quote	What You Thinks This Means
"Ma was thinking about him all the time and she did not like to talk about it."	

Response Notes

ON THE BANKS OF PLUM CREEK
(continued)

"The time will go faster," she said, "if we think of other things."

All day Saturday they hoped that Mr. Nelson was finding a letter from Pa at the post-office in town. Laura and Jack went far along the prairie road to wait for Mr. Nelson's wagon. The grasshoppers had eaten everything, and now they were going away, not in one big cloud as they had come, but in little, short-

© GREAT SOURCE. COPYING IS PROHIBITED.

ON THE BANKS OF PLUM CREEK
(continued)

flying clouds. Still, millions of grasshoppers were left.

There was no letter from Pa. "Never mind," Ma said. "One will come."

Once when Laura was slowly coming up the <u>knoll</u> without a letter, she thought, "Suppose no letter ever comes?"

She tried not to think that again. But she did. One day she looked at Mary and knew that Mary was thinking it, too.

knoll—little hill.

© GREAT SOURCE. COPYING IS PROHIBITED.

That night Laura could not bear it any longer. She asked Ma, "Pa will come home, won't he?"

"Of course, Pa will come home!" Ma exclaimed. Then Laura and Mary knew that Ma, too, was afraid that something had happened to Pa.

Perhaps his boots had fallen to pieces and he was limping barefooted. Perhaps <u>cattle</u> had hurt him. Perhaps a train had hit him. He had not taken his gun; perhaps wolves had got him. Maybe in dark woods at night a <u>panther</u> had leaped on him from a tree.

cattle (cat•tle)—cows, bulls, and oxen.
panther (pan•ther)—large wild cat, like a
    mountain lion.

© GREAT SOURCE. COPYING IS PROHIBITED.

DOUBLE-ENTRY JOURNAL

Quote	What You Thinks This Means
"She asked Ma, 'Pa will come home, won't he?' "	

ON THE BANKS OF PLUM CREEK
(continued)

Response Notes

The next Saturday afternoon, when Laura and Jack were starting to meet Mr. Nelson, she saw him coming across the footbridge. Something white was in his hand. Laura flew down the knoll. The white thing was a letter.

"Oh, thank you! Thank you!" Laura said. She ran to the house so fast that she could not breathe. Ma was washing Carrie's face. She took the letter in her shaking wet hands, and sat down.

© GREAT SOURCE. COPYING IS PROHIBITED.

"It's from Pa," she said. Her hand shook so she could hardly take a hairpin from her hair. She slit the envelope and <u>drew</u> out the letter. She unfolded it, and there was a piece of paper money.

"Pa's all right," Ma said. She snatched her apron up to her face and cried.

Her wet face came out of the apron shining with joy. She kept wiping her eyes while she read the letter to Mary and Laura.

drew—pulled out.

© GREAT SOURCE. COPYING IS PROHIBITED.

ON THE BANKS OF PLUM CREEK
(continued)

Pa had had to walk three hundred miles before he found a job. Now he was working in the wheat-fields and getting a dollar a day. He sent Ma five dollars and kept three for new boots. Crops were good where he was, and if Ma and the girls were making out all right, he would stay there as long as the work lasted.

They missed him and wanted him to come home. But he was safe, and already he had new boots. They were very happy that day.

DOUBLE-ENTRY JOURNAL

Quote	What You Thinks This Means
"Pa had to walk three hundred miles before he found a job."	

Reread *On the Banks of Plum Creek*. On this reading, be sure you have responded to each quote in the **Double-entry Journals.**

© GREAT SOURCE. COPYING IS PROHIBITED.

WORD WORK

Some **compound words** have 3 syllables or beats. It's easy to say these long words if you know how to divide them into syllables. Follow these rules:

Rule #1: Divide the compound word into 2 small words.

Rule #2: Divide the small word that has 2 syllables by putting a line between the 2 consonant letters in the middle of the word.

Example: grasshoppers = grass / hoppers   (Rule 1)

Example: grasshoppers = grass / hop / pers   (Rule 2)

1. Divide each word below into syllables by following Rule 1 and Rule 2.
2. Pratice saying each word and think of how you could use it in a sentence.

Word	Divided into Syllables
membership	
headquarters	
midwinter	
jellyfish	
underground	
blueberry	

READING REMINDER
Making pictures in your head and seeing the people, places, and action helps you understand and remember a story.

© GREAT SOURCE. COPYING IS PROHIBITED.

III. GET READY TO WRITE

A. BRAINSTORM

On the Banks of Plum Creek tells about an important time for Laura and her family. Think about some important events for you and your family.

1. Write the name of your family in the center of the web.
2. Brainstorm 3–4 important events for your family.

© GREAT SOURCE. COPYING IS PROHIBITED.

B. GATHER DETAILS

Get ready to write an autobiographical paragraph. It will tell about an important event that happened to you or your family.

1. On the web on page 177, circle the event that you would most like to tell about.
2. Write the event in the center of the story star and answer the questions.

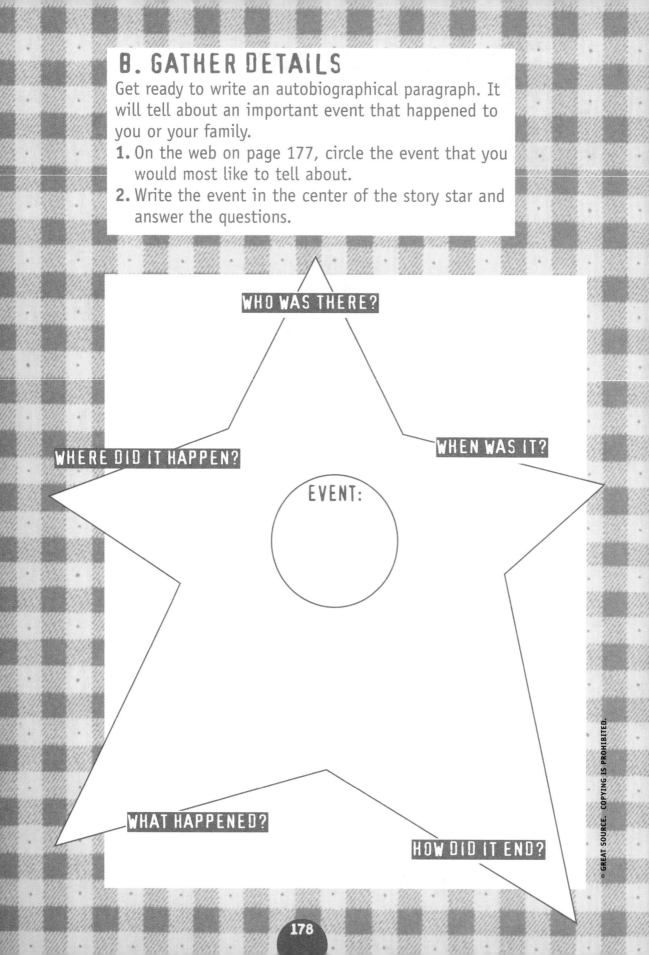

WHO WAS THERE?

WHEN WAS IT?

WHERE DID IT HAPPEN?

EVENT:

WHAT HAPPENED?

HOW DID IT END?

© GREAT SOURCE. COPYING IS PROHIBITED.

WRITE

Now you are ready to write an **autobiographical paragraph** about an important event for you and your family.

1. Begin by explaining when the event happened.
2. Then explain what happened. Use your story star to help you tell about the experience.
3. In the last sentence, say how it ended and how you felt.
4. Use the Writers' Checklist to edit your paragraph.

Title: _____

_____

_____

_____

_____

_____

_____

_____

_____

_____

_____

_____

_____

_____

_____

_____

_____

_____

© GREAT SOURCE. COPYING IS PROHIBITED.

Continue writing on the next page.

Continue your paragraph.

....

....

....

....

....

....

....

....

....

WRITERS' CHECKLIST

Apostrophes

☐ **Did you add an 's to form the possessive of singular nouns? Possessive nouns show ownership.**
EXAMPLES: *Pa's letter, the car's color, Luis's opinion*

V. LOOK BACK

What did *On the Banks of Plum Creek* mean to you? Write your thoughts below.

Think about Your Reading
READERS' CHECKLIST

Meaning

☐ **Did you learn something from the reading?**
☐ **Did you have a strong feeling about one part of the reading?**

© GREAT SOURCE. COPYING IS PROHIBITED.

15

Ramona's World

What makes a story funny? Sometimes when a character has a big problem, it can be funny. Ramona is helping to take care of her little sister, but she is headed for big trouble. What is she going to do?

© GREAT SOURCE. COPYING IS PROHIBITED.

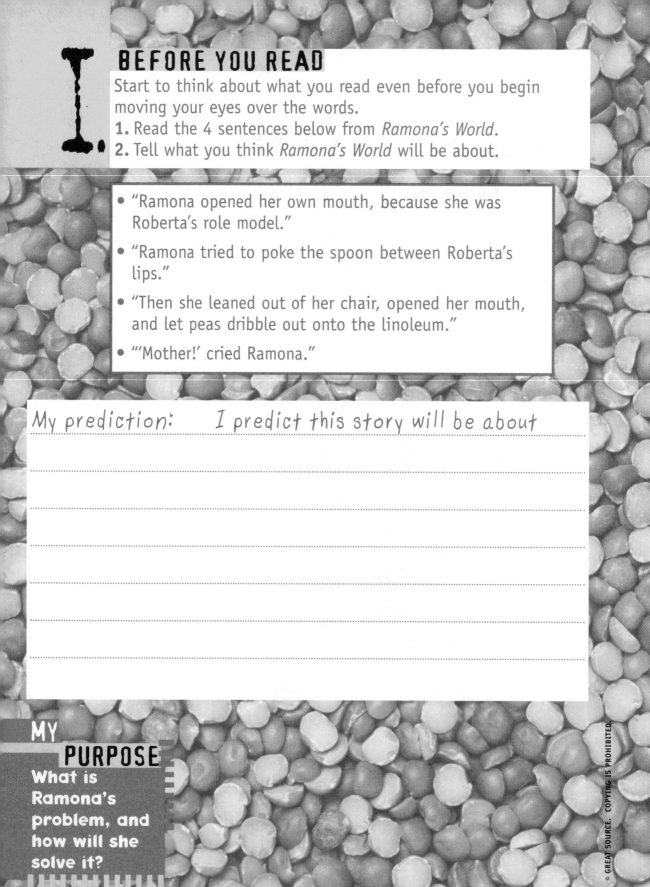

I. BEFORE YOU READ

Start to think about what you read even before you begin moving your eyes over the words.

1. Read the 4 sentences below from *Ramona's World*.

2. Tell what you think *Ramona's World* will be about.

- "Ramona opened her own mouth, because she was Roberta's role model."
- "Ramona tried to poke the spoon between Roberta's lips."
- "Then she leaned out of her chair, opened her mouth, and let peas dribble out onto the linoleum."
- "'Mother!' cried Ramona."

My prediction: I predict this story will be about

MY PURPOSE

What is Ramona's problem, and how will she solve it?

© GREAT SOURCE. COPYING IS PROHIBITED.

II. READ

Read this part of *Ramona's World*.

1. On your first reading, underline parts of the story that tell you about Ramona's problem.

2. Then read the story again. This time write comments in the Notes that **make clear** what Ramona does.

Ramona's World by Beverly Cleary

Ramona dipped up a spoonful of cottage cheese. "Open wide," she said to Roberta. "Down the little red lane." That was what her mother said when she fed Roberta. <u>Ramona opened her own mouth, because she was Roberta's <u>role model</u>. Roberta <u>obediently</u> <u>imitated</u> her and accepted the cottage cheese. "Good girl," said Ramona. Roberta smiled a messy smile and pounded her heels against the high chair.

role model (role mod•el)—person whom others look up to and try to act like.
obediently (o•be•di•ent•ly)—doing what is asked.
imitated (im•i•tat•ed)—copied.

Response Notes

EXAMPLE:

Ramona does what she wants Roberta to do.

© GREAT SOURCE. COPYING IS PROHIBITED.

Mrs. Quimby was saying, "I really enjoy our book club. Now that I am no longer working—not that looking after my daughters isn't work—I enjoy exercising my brain."

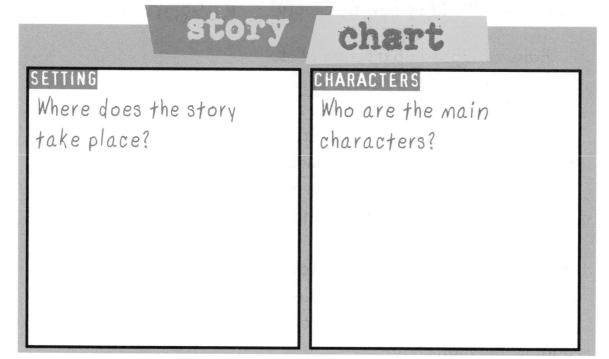

story chart

SETTING	CHARACTERS
Where does the story take place?	Who are the main characters?

Ramona was surprised and a little hurt that her mother found her daughters work. Roberta reached for the spoon. Ramona held on to it because Roberta would finish faster if she was fed.

© GREAT SOURCE. COPYING IS PROHIBITED.

RAMONA'S WORLD (continued)

Ramona tried strained peas next. "Come on, Roberta. Down the hatch," she said, using her father's words.

The hatch remained closed. Ramona tried to poke the spoon between Roberta's lips. Roberta did not care to be poked. She began to look stubborn. Ramona was growing impatient to get to the television. If the husband of Blond Nurse found out about Curly-haired Doctor—

Roberta kept her lips tightly closed. "Look, Roberta. Watch your big sister." Ramona opened her mouth wide, and after thinking it over, Roberta did the same. Ramona popped the peas into her mouth. Roberta frowned but accepted another spoonful. Then she leaned out of her chair, opened her

strained peas—peas that are smoothed out so small children can eat them.
impatient (im•pa•tient)—not wanting to wait.

© GREAT SOURCE. COPYING IS PROHIBITED.

mouth, and let peas <u>dribble</u> out onto the <u>linoleum</u>.

"Roberta!" cried Ramona. When

story chart

PROBLEM

What is the problem?

Roberta looked worried, she changed the tone of her voice and said, "Yum-yum. Nice peas full of vitamins and good things." She smiled as she held a <u>generous</u> spoonful to Roberta's lips and thought, <u>Horrid</u>, nasty peas, before

dribble (drib•ble)—fall from the mouth.
linoleum (lin•o•le•um)—washable material used in covering floors and counters.
generous (gen•er•ous)—larger than usual.
Horrid (hor•rid)—very bad.

© GREAT SOURCE. COPYING IS PROHIBITED.

RAMONA'S WORLD (continued)

she said, "Open wide." When Roberta did as she was told, Ramona spooned in the peas.

With her mouth full of peas, Roberta looked both surprised and disappointed, as if her sister had betrayed her. Then she blew hard, spraying mushy, squishy, smelly green peas all over Ramona.

"Roberta!" cried Ramona, dropping the spoon on the high-chair tray and wiping her face on her sleeve. Roberta picked up the spoon, beat it in her food, and <u>crowed</u>. Then, filled with <u>glee</u> at

crowed—shouted happily.
glee—happiness.

© GREAT SOURCE. COPYING IS PROHIBITED.

what she had done, she threw the spoon on the floor. Why bother with it when she had hands? She patted her food and rubbed her hair.

"Mother!" cried Ramona. "Roberta's making a mess."

"<u>Cope</u>, dear. I'm busy," answered Mrs. Quimby from the hall. "Just do the best you can."

Cope—deal with a problem.

story chart

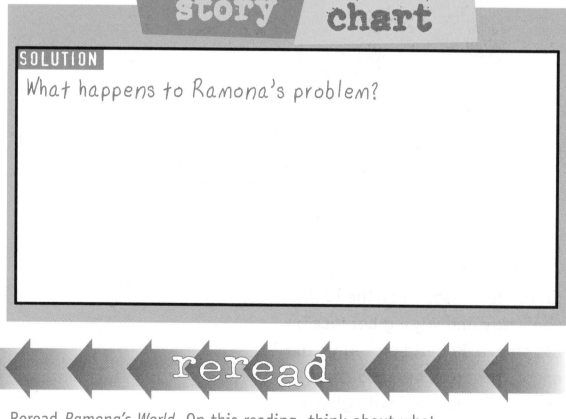

SOLUTION

What happens to Ramona's problem?

reread

Reread *Ramona's World*. On this reading, think about what Ramona did and be sure you have completed the **Story Chart** organizers.

© GREAT SOURCE. COPYING IS PROHIBITED.

WORD WORK

Many words end in a consonant letter before a **y**. It can be tricky to add suffixes to these words. The **y** changes to an **i** when you add some suffixes or endings that start with a vowel.

nosy + er = *nosier*   lazy + est = *laziest*

1. Add suffixes or endings to the words below.
2. Remember to change the **y** to an **i** before you add the suffix. One has been done for you.

Word	+ Suffix/Ending	New Word
creepy	+ est	creepiest
busy	+ est	
sleepy	+ er	
cozy	+ est	
noisy	+ er	
easy	+ est	

© GREAT SOURCE. COPYING IS PROHIBITED.

READING REMINDER

Predicting before you read helps you get into the story and understand it better.

III. GET READY TO WRITE

A. REMEMBER DETAILS

Did you think that Ramona's story is funny? Think about the things that Ramona does to get Roberta to eat. Think about what Roberta does.

1. Use the storyboards below to tell Ramona's story.

2. Write a phrase or sentence in each box.

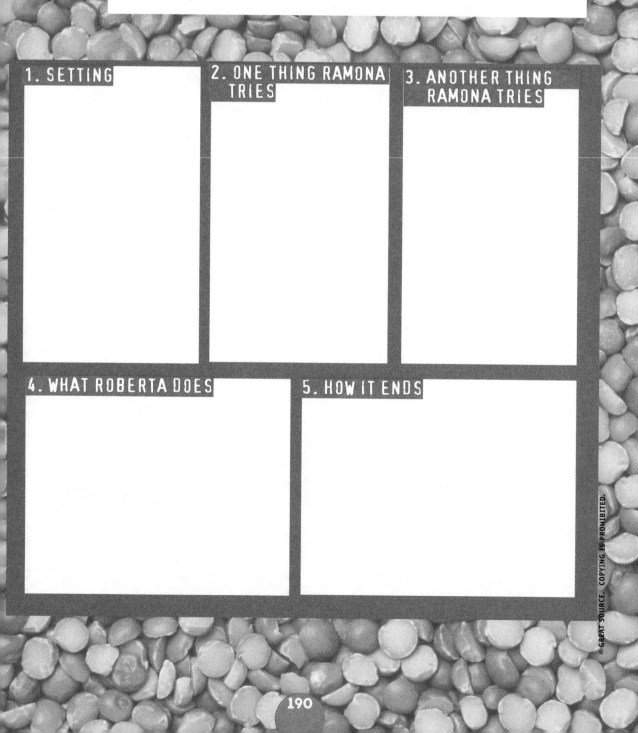

1. SETTING

2. ONE THING RAMONA TRIES

3. ANOTHER THING RAMONA TRIES

4. WHAT ROBERTA DOES

5. HOW IT ENDS

© GREAT SOURCE. COPYING IS PROHIBITED.

B. WRITE A TOPIC SENTENCE

Get ready to write a summary paragraph telling what happened to Ramona.

1. Write a topic sentence for your paragraph. In your own words, say what Ramona is trying to do.
2. Use the example to give you an idea of what to say.

Example: Ramona has a hard time trying to feed her baby sister.

My topic sentence:

C. PLAN

Organize your paragraph into 3 parts: a beginning, a middle, and an end. Use your notes from page 190 to help you.

Beginning

Middle

End

© GREAT SOURCE. COPYING IS PROHIBITED.

IV. WRITE

Now you are ready to write a **summary** telling what happened to Ramona.

1. First write your topic sentence.
2. Use your plan on page 191 to help you. Start a new sentence for each detail.
3. Use the Writers' Checklist to edit your summary.

Summary of <u>Ramona's World</u>

Continue writing on the next page.

© GREAT SOURCE. COPYING IS PROHIBITED.

© GREAT SOURCE. COPYING IS PROHIBITED.

WRITERS' CHECKLIST

Commas

☐ **Did you use a comma and a conjunction (*and, or, but, so*) in your compound sentences?**

EXAMPLES: *Roberta was stubborn, and she wouldn't eat. Ramona kept trying, but she was frustrated.*

V. LOOK BACK

Would you recommend *Ramona's World* to a friend? Why or why not? Write your thoughts below.

....

....

....

Think about Your Reading

READERS' CHECKLIST
Enjoyment

☐ **Did you like the reading?**

☐ **Would you recommend the reading to a friend?**

194

© GREAT SOURCE. COPYING IS PROHIBITED.

16

The Polar Regions

The Earth has many different climates. In the rain forests, the weather is warm and rainy. In the deserts, it is hot and dry. But near the ends of the Earth, it gets colder than you can imagine. What can survive in that kind of cold?

© GREAT SOURCE. COPYING IS PROHIBITED.

BEFORE YOU READ

Gather your thoughts on a subject before you begin to read. One way to do that is with a web.

1. With a partner, discuss the words *north pole* and *south pole*. What do they mean to you? What do they mean to your partner?
2. List words, phrases, or places that you think of when you hear the words *north pole* and *south pole*.
3. Write your ideas on the lines below.

north pole
south pole

MY
PURPOSE

What is it like at the north and south poles, and who or what lives there?

GREAT SOURCE. COPYING IS PROHIBITED.

I. ## READ

Read these parts of the book called *The Polar Regions*.
1. On your first reading, circle parts of the story that make you wonder about life at the north and south poles.
2. On your next reading, write in the Notes the **questions** that popped into your head.
3. When you find an answer, write that too.

The Polar Regions
by Mel Higginson

THE POLAR REGIONS

The poles are imaginary points at the "ends" of the Earth. The north pole is in the Far North, in a region known as the Arctic. The south pole is in the Far South, at the opposite end of the Earth. The south pole is on the continent of Antarctica.

The polar regions—the areas near the poles—are the Earth's <u>iceboxes</u>. They are extremely cold in winter. Both polar regions have <u>rugged</u> mountains, lots of ice and amazing numbers of tough animals.

iceboxes (ice•box•es)—boxes filled with ice to store food; freezers.
rugged (rug•ged)—having a rough surface or outline.

Response Notes

EXAMPLE:
How cold is it during the summer?

© GREAT SOURCE. COPYING IS PROHIBITED.

197

THE ARCTIC

The Arctic region is not a continent. It is an area that includes the Arctic Ocean and parts of Canada, Alaska, Greenland, Russia and far northern Europe. Arctic land is covered by a "carpet" of low-lying plants called Arctic tundra.

Arctic winters are dark and <u>frigid</u>. Spring, however, brings an explosion of plant and animal life. Hundreds of thousands of birds migrate, or travel, to the Arctic to nest. Whales migrate to the Arctic seas to <u>feed</u>.

frigid (frig•id)—very cold.
feed—eat.

stop and think

What 3 things have you learned about the Arctic?

© GREAT SOURCE. COPYING IS PROHIBITED.

THE POLAR REGIONS (continued)

ANTARCTICA

Antarctica is a continent almost covered by ice and snow. Only a tiny part of Antarctica is fit for living things. Most of those <u>organisms</u> are simple plants and tiny animals.

Near Antarctica, though, the islands and seas are rich with life. Thousands of whales and seals live in the Antarctic region. Millions of sea birds, many of them penguins, live there in huge groups called colonies.

ANIMALS OF THE POLAR REGIONS

Marine, or sea, mammals— whales and seals—live in both polar regions.

No land mammals live in the Antarctic region. However, polar bears, caribou, hares, lemmings and musk oxen live in the Arctic.

Both polar regions have huge numbers of birds. Antarctica is famous for penguins, but more than 40 other kinds of birds live in the region, too.

organisms (or•gan•isms)—living things.

© GREAT SOURCE. COPYING IS PROHIBITED.

HOW ANIMALS LIVE IN POLAR REGIONS

The animals of polar regions have special ways to deal with living in such cold habitats, or homes.

Nearly all marine mammals, and some birds, have a layer of fat called blubber. Blubber helps animals store energy and stay warm. The blood of some polar animals has a warming chemical in it.

stop and think

How do animals deal with the cold in the Arctic and in Antarctica?

© GREAT SOURCE. COPYING IS PROHIBITED.

THE POLAR REGIONS (continued)

The Arctic fox has short ears and a short nose. That means less of its body is exposed to the cold.

PEOPLE IN THE ARCTIC

Groups of people have lived in the Arctic region for thousands of years. Eskimos are the best-known and most widespread group.

Until recent years, Eskimos lived off the Arctic lands and seas. They had to hunt and fish for most of their food. They made boats of animal skins and weapons from bones.

Today, most Arctic people live with both modern ways and old ways.

stop and think

How do the Eskimos survive in the Arctic?

reread

Reread *The Polar Regions*. As you read it again, think about some of the facts you learned. Be sure you have answered all of the **Stop and Think** questions.

© GREAT SOURCE. COPYING IS PROHIBITED.

WORD WORK

Below are long words made by adding **prefixes** and **suffixes** to **base words** from *The Polar Regions*.

1. Cross out the prefix, suffix, or both on each word.
2. Then find the base word. You might need to add a *silent e*.
3. Write the base word under the heading below. An example has been done for you.

Word	Base Word
~~un~~end~~ing~~	end
intercontinental	
reliving	
layering	
modernize	
rewarmed	
migrating	

4. With a partner, take turns saying each base word and then the longer form of the word.

READING REMINDER
Asking questions about new information can help you better remember new facts.

© GREAT SOURCE. COPYING IS PROHIBITED.

III. GET READY TO WRITE

A. ORGANIZE INFORMATION

Prepare to write a summary. First, you need to find the main topics in *The Polar Regions*.

1. *The Polar Regions* talks about 6 big topics. Each one is the name of a heading. Fill in the small boxes with the headings. Two have been done for you.
2. Then, on the dotted lines below, write 1 thing the author says about each topic.

The Polar Regions

1. The Polar Regions

2. The Arctic

3.

4.

5.

6.

© GREAT SOURCE. COPYING IS PROHIBITED.

B. FIND THE MAIN IDEA

Choose the heading that most interests you to be the subject of your summary.

1. Write the author's main idea about the subject in a sentence of your own.
2. List 3 details that you can find that support the main idea.
3. Then end by telling what you think about the subject.

Your subject: _____

Sentence with main idea:
....
....
....

Detail 1:
....
....

Detail 2:
....
....

Detail 3:
....
....

Closing sentence:
....
....

© GREAT SOURCE. COPYING IS PROHIBITED.

IV. WRITE

Use your notes from the previous page to write a **summary** of part of *The Polar Regions*.

1. Begin with the main idea sentence. That is the topic sentence.
2. Then give 3 details that support your main idea.
3. End with a closing sentence that restates your main idea and tells what you think about the subject.
4. Use the Writers' Checklist to help you edit your summary.

My Summary

Continue writing on the next page.

GREAT SOURCE. COPYING IS PROHIBITED.

Continue your summary.

....

....

....

....

....

....

....

....

WRITERS' CHECKLIST

Apostrophes

☐ **Did you add an apostrophe (') to form the possessive of plural nouns that end in *s*?**
EXAMPLES: *polar bears' claws, scientists' books*

☐ **Did you add 's to form the possessive of plural nouns that do not end in *s*?** EXAMPLES: *the women's room, the deer's tails*

LOOK BACK

What would you tell a friend about *The Polar Regions*?
Write your ideas below.

....

....

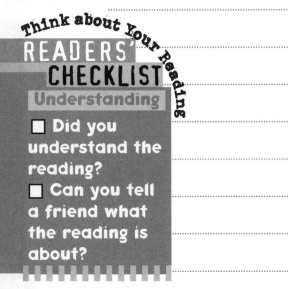

Think about Your Reading

READERS' CHECKLIST

Understanding

☐ **Did you understand the reading?**
☐ **Can you tell a friend what the reading is about?**

....

....

....

....

....

....

© GREAT SOURCE. COPYING IS PROHIBITED.

Acknowledgments

6–10, "Blossoms," "Summer," "Prayer," "Love That Boy," by Walter Dean Myers, from BROWN ANGELS. Copyright © 1993 by Walter Dean Myers. Used by permission of HarperCollins Publishers.

15 *George Washington Carver* from GEORGE WASHINGTON CARVER by Patricia and Fredrick McKissack. Copyright © 1991 by Enslow Publishers. Reprinted by permission of Enslow Publishers.

25 *Tornado*, by Betsy Byars. Text copyright © 1996 by Betsy Byars. Used by permission of HarperCollins Publishers.

39 *Baseball Saved Us,* by Ken Mochizuki. BASEBALL SAVED US text copyright © 1993 by Ken Mochizuki. Permission granted by Lee & Low Books, Inc.

51 "Feathers," by Joseph Bruchac. "Feathers" reprinted by permission of Barbara S. Kouts, agent.

53 "The Hurricane," from SING TO THE SUN. Copyright © 1992 by Ashley Bryan. Used by permission of HarperCollins Publishers.

63 *Ant Cities*, by Arthur Dorros. Copyright © 1978 by Arthur Dorros. Used by permission of HarperCollins Publishers.

73 *Easter Parade* from EASTER PARADE by Eloise Greenfield. Text © 1998 by Eloise Greenfield. Illustrations © 1998 by Jan Spivey Gilchrist. Reprinted by permission of Hyperion Books for Children.

85 *Vanished! The Mysterious Disappearance of Amelia Earhart* from VANISHED! THE MYSTERIOUS DISAPPEARANCE OF AMELIA EARHART by Monica Kulling. Copyright © 1996 by Monica Kulling. Reprinted by permission of Random House Children's Books, a division of Random House, Inc.

97 *Hiroshima*, by Laurence Yep. from HIROSHIMA. Copyright © 1995 by Laurence Yep. Reprinted by permission of Scholastic Inc.

109 *Black Star, Bright Dawn* excerpt from BLACK STAR, BRIGHT DAWN. Copyright © 1988 by Scott O'Dell. Reprinted by permission of Houghton Mifflin Company. All rights reserved.

121 *Animal Fact/Animal Fable,* from *ANIMAL FACT/ANIMAL FABLES* by Seymour Simon. Copyright © 1979 by Seymour Simon. Reprinted by permission of Crown Children's Books, a division of Random House, Inc.

133 *Very Last First Time* excerpt from VERY LAST FIRST TIME. Text copyright © 1985 by Jan Andrews. First published in Canada by Groundwood Books/Douglas & McIntyre Ltd. Reprinted by permission of the publisher.

145 *If You Lived with the Sioux Indians* Copyright © 1972 by Ann McGovern. Excerpt from IF YOU LIVED WITH THE SIOUX INDIANS, published by Scholastic, Inc. Reprinted by permission of Curtis Brown, Ltd.

157 *John Henry*, from JOHN HENRY by Julius Lester. Copyright © 1994 by Julius Lester. Used by permission of Dial Books for Young Readers, an imprint of Penguin Putnam books for Young Readers, a division of Penguin Putnam Inc.

169 *On the Banks of Plum Creek* from ON THE BANKS OF PLUM CREEK by Laura Ingalls Wilder. Text copyright © 1937 by Laura Ingalls Wilder renewed © 1965 by Roger L. MacBride. Illustrations copyright © 1953 by Garth Williams. Used by permission of HarperCollins Publishers.

183 *Ramona's World,* by Beverly Cleary. Text copyright © 1999 by Beverly Cleary. Used by permission of HarperCollins Publishers.

197 *The Polar Regions* © 1994 The Rourke Corporation.

Photography:
COVER: All photos © Eileen Ryan.
TABLE OF CONTENTS and INTRODUCTION: All photos © Eileen Ryan except where noted.

Illustration:
Chapter One: Holladay, Reggie
Chapter Two: Jones, Tim
Chapter Three: Stergulz, Rich
Chapter Four: Hullinger, CD
Chapter Five: Dammer, Mike
Chapter Seven: Canaday, Ralph
Chapter Eight: Pollema-Cahill, Phyllis
Chapter Nine: Wendland, Paula
Chapter Ten: Kennedy, Victor
Chapter Twelve: Teare, Brad
Chapter Sixteen: Bittner-Howard, Linda

Cover and Book Design: Christine Ronan, Sean O'Neill, and Maria Mariottini, Ronan Design
Permissions:
Feldman and Associates
Developed by Nieman Inc.

The editors have made every effort to trace the ownership of all copyrighted selections found in this book and to make full acknowledgment for their use. Omissions brought to our attention will be corrected in a subsequent edition.

©GREAT SOURCE. COPYING IS PROHIBITED.

Author/Title **Index**

©GREAT SOURCE. COPYING IS PROHIBITED.

W9-BRN-163

Nancy Casias
576-9681

READY
RESOURCE
for
RELIEF
SOCIETY

The

READY
RESOURCE
for
RELIEF
SOCIETY

Volume Two

TEACHINGS OF PRESIDENTS OF THE
CHURCH: SPENCER W. KIMBALL

compiled by

KIMBERLY S. SHAFFER

CFI
Springville, Utah

© 2007 Kimberly S. Shaffer
All rights reserved.

No part of this book may be reproduced in any form whatsoever, whether by graphic, visual, electronic, film, microfilm, tape recording, or any other means, without prior written permission of the publisher, except in the case of brief passages embodied in critical reviews and articles.

ISBN 13: 978-1-55517-981-6
ISBN 10: 1-55517-981-9

Published by CFI, an imprint of Cedar Fort, Inc., 2373 W. 700 S., Springville, UT, 84663
Distributed by Cedar Fort, Inc. www.cedarfort.com

LIBRARY OF CONGRESS CATALOGING-IN-PUBLICATION DATA

A resource guide for Relief Society / compiled by Kimberly S. Shaffer.
    p. cm.
  ISBN-13: 978-1-55517-981-6
    1. Christian life--Mormon authors. 2. Church of Jesus Christ of Latter-day Saints--Doctrines. 3. Mormon Church--Doctrines. 4. Relief Society (Church of Jesus Christ of Latter-day Saints) I. Shaffer, Kimberly S. II. Title.

  BX8656.R435 2007
  248.4'89332--dc22

                          2006032438

Cover and book design by Nicole Williams
Cover design © 2007 by Lyle Mortimer

Printed in the United States of America

10 9 8 7 6 5 4 3 2 1

Printed on acid-free paper

DEDICATION

For GG—*the writer.*

CONTENTS

ACKNOWLEDGMENTS

Thanks to Heather Holm, Annaliese Cox,
and Kimiko Hammari for their editing; Nikki
Williams for the cover; the staff at Cedar Fort for
publishing this book; and, most important,
my family.

INTRODUCTION

The Ready Resource for Relief Society is intended to help making preparing lessons both easier and less stressful. Each chapter includes hymns appropriate for the lesson, quick summaries of the Church manual, and quotes to supplement your class discussions. In addition, each chapter contains a space to take notes and a handout. The dotted line around each handout equals the same size as half a sheet of paper so copying is quick and easy.

LESSON ONE

TO LIVE WITH HIM SOMEDAY

Hymns

No. 301, "I am a Child of God"
No. 302, "I Know My Father Lives"
No. 304, "Teach Me to Walk in the Light"

SUMMARY:

1. In the pre-mortal life, we were taught the plan of salvation and entered into a covenant with Heavenly Father. We were promised a physical body, and we, in turn, promised to progress toward perfection and try our best to be like Him. We were taught that our life was made up of three parts: pre-mortal life, mortal life, and immortality. In addition, we taught that these segments are not individually exclusive. Our choices in one segment will directly affect the outcome in the next segment. Furthermore, we understood our purpose of our earthly lives, and we knew what we were getting into. We knew that there might be sorrow, pain, and heartache, but we also knew what waited for us if we were faithful and followed the plan.

2. Everyone living on this earth made the proper choice in our first estate and was given the gift of a physical body. We must remember that we are not just on this earth to have "fun." We made a promise in the pre-mortal life, and we have to uphold that promise.

Procrastination is one of the most serious vices in human life and takes a huge toll on our earthly lives. Therefore, procrastination must have an even more lasting and devastating effect on our spiritual lives. We must begin now to uphold that promise and progress toward perfection; this can only be done through the gospel of Jesus Christ. This gospel and its ordinances provide the path through this second stage of life and into immortality. We need to remember that repentance is an integral part of this path and that God is eager for us to repent and exercise self-control and keep His commandments.

3. The third stage of life is immortality. There is a difference between immortality and eternal life, and those who follow the path previously discussed will receive eternal life, which is exaltation in the highest kingdom of heaven. Not everyone will reach exaltation. In fact, only a few will reach that highest degree of glory. This is not because the opportunity was not available, but rather, it is because not many are willing to put forth the effort it takes to gain eternal life. Many members of the Church feel that if they are baptized, endowed, and sealed in the temple, they are guaranteed eternal life. This is not the case. We need to remember that in addition to these things, we must also keep the commandments and overcome our weaknesses and temptations.

QUOTES:

"God did not send you here to fail. He did not give you life to waste it. He bestowed upon you the gift of mortality that you might gain experience—positive, wonderful, purposeful experience—that will lead to life eternal" (Gordon B. Hinckley, *Stand a Little Taller*, Eagle Gate, Salt Lake City, Utah, 2001, 365).

"The Lord has carefully provided a plan of life called the plan of salvation. It comprises all of the laws, ordinances, principles, and doctrines required to complete our mortal journey and progress to a state of exaltation enjoyed by our Father in Heaven" (Duane B. Gerrard, "The Plan of Salvation: A Flight Plan for Life," *Ensign*, Nov. 1997, 77).

"The plan is a most stunning example of the precious perspective of the gospel of Jesus Christ. Furthermore, full faith in the Lord Jesus Christ includes and requires full faith in His Father's plan of salvation" (Neal A. Maxwell, "The Great Plan of the Eternal God," *Ensign*, May 1984, 21).

NOTES:

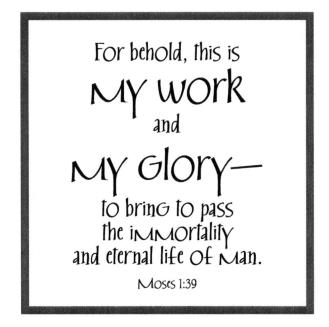

For behold, this is

MY WORK

and

MY GLORY—

to bring to pass
the immortality
and eternal life of man.

Moses 1:39

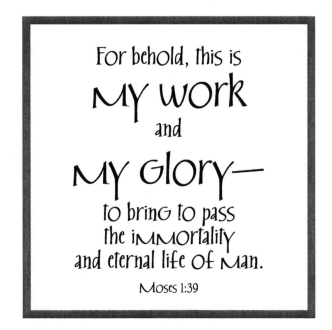

For behold, this is

MY WORK

and

MY GLORY—

to bring to pass
the immortality
and eternal life of man.

Moses 1:39

LESSON TWO

TRAGEDY
OR
DESTINY

Hymns

No. 129, "Where Can I Turn for Peace?"
No. 124, "Be Still My Soul"
No. 115, "Come, Ye Disconsolate"

SUMMARY:

1. When faced with tragedy, we often wonder why the Lord allows bad things to happen. The Lord has the power to prevent tragedy and has the power to control our lives, but if He were to do that for us, it would take away our free agency. If we didn't understand that life is eternal, tragedy would be near unbearable; however, because we can keep an eternal perspective, we understand that tragedy in our lives is often a faith building experience. Adversity can humble us and teach us to be more reliant upon God; if God were to remove adversity from our lives, it would nullify the plan prepared for us, and we would have no way to progress and grow.

2. Because our judgment and knowledge is so limited, we often feel that early death is a disaster or tragedy. This attitude reflects the idea that we believe life on earth is more preferable than coming closer to exaltation. Furthermore, members of the Church have responsibilities on this side of the veil as well as on the other side of the veil. Many people have died without the knowledge of the

gospel, and those faithful and righteous spirits who have passed on are marshaled in ranks to carry the message of the gospel to those who have yet to hear the message of light and truth.

3. While we understand and acknowledge that death can open doors of opportunity, we are usually not prepared for it, and we often do not wish it for our loved ones. The priesthood can heal those who have sufficient faith, if it is not their appointed time to die. Also, we can prevent ourselves from passing on before our time if we take proper care of our bodies and live accordingly to God's plan.

We knew before we came to earth that there would be heartache and sorrow and that we would die. However terrible these things may seem to us, we need to remember that we were eager for the opportunity to come to earth even if our life here would be short. When we keep an eternal perspective and trust in God, we understand that He has a plan for each and every one of us even if that plan involves sorrow and tragedy.

QUOTES:

"Tragedy and frustration are the unexpected intruders on life's plans. Someone has said, 'Life is what happens to you while you are making other plans.' It is important that we not look upon our afflictions as a punishment from God. True, our own actions may cause some of our problems, but often there is no evident misconduct that has caused our trials. Just the normal journey through life teaches us that nothing worthwhile comes easy" (Marvin J. Ashton, "If Thou Endure It Well," *Ensign*, Nov. 1984, 20).

"I believe we all understood that by coming to earth, we would be exposed to all of the experiences of earth life, including the not-so-pleasant trials of pain, suffering, hopelessness, sin, and death. There would be opposition and adversity. And if that was all we knew about the plan, I doubt if any of us would have embraced it, rejoicing, 'That's what I have always wanted—pain, suffering, hopelessness, sin, and death.' But it all came into focus, and it became acceptable, even desirable, when an Elder Brother stepped forward and offered that He would go down and make it all right. Out of pain and suffering He would bring peace. Out of hopelessness He would bring hope. Out of transgression He would bring repentance and forgiveness. Out of death He would bring the resurrection of lives. And with that explanation and most generous offer, each and every one of us concluded, 'I can do that. That is a risk worth taking.' And so we chose" (Richard C. Edgley, "For Thy Good," *Ensign*, May 2002, 65).

"Part of the answer is that without opposition and testing, free agency loses its meaning. Opposition, tribulation, afflictions, the refining fire are part of the eternal plan" (Marion D. Hanks, "I Will Look unto the Lord," *Ensign*, Nov. 1986, 11).

NOTES:

Five Ways I Can Keep an ETERNAL PERSPECTIVE When I Am Faced With ADVERSITY OR TRAGEDY

1 _____

_____

2 _____

_____

3 _____

_____

4 _____

_____

5 _____

_____

LESSON THREE

JESUS CHRIST,
MY SAVIOR, MY LORD

Hymns

No. 93, "I Stand All Amazed"
No. 6, "Redeemer of Israel"
No. 134, "I Believe in Christ"

SUMMARY:

1. We know that Jesus Christ was a great man, teacher, and philanthropist. We also know that He is the son of God and the Savior of all mankind. The scriptures bear witness to His glory and power. The scriptures also bear record of His earthly and pre-mortal ministry. We learn through the scriptures that Jesus Christ was the creator of this earth and the author of the plan of salvation. He is also the Redeemer of mankind and the liaison between us and the Father.

2. The Atonement of Jesus Christ offers two very important factors. First, the Atonement saves all men from the Fall. The Fall ensures that each person who comes to this earth will experience a physical death. Through the Atonement, Christ overcame death and was resurrected, making it possible for every living man to be reunited with his or her body after death. Secondly, the Atonement saves the penitent and repentant from personal sin. Christ is the Redeemer of mankind and has paid the price for all the sins of the world.

Justice will be satisfied whether we partake of the Atonement and repent. If we do not take advantage of this gift, Christ will have suffered in vain. The Atonement is the only way to eternal life, and it is free to all men who are willing to repent and come unto Christ and live as He did.

3. Christ showed perfect love when He sacrificed His life for us. We can show our love for Him by following His gospel. When we repent of our sins and come unto Christ, He is pleased with us. Christ and Heavenly Father find joy when we acknowledge their hands in our lives and when we keep their commandments. We too, can feel this joy when we keep the commandments and take advantage of the Atonement. The Atonement can bring us great hope and joy. It allows us to have life eternal and it frees us from the bonds of sin. Without the Atonement, we would not have the opportunity to live after death. Because of this great sacrifice, we can be together in the eternities and feel even more joy than is possible on this earth.

QUOTES:

"Jesus Christ is the light and life of the world because all things were made by him. Under the direction and according to the plan of God the Father, Jesus Christ is the Creator, the source of the light and life of all things. Through modern revelation we have the testimony of John, who bore record that Jesus Christ is 'the light and the Redeemer of the world, the Spirit of truth, who came into the world, because the world was made by him, and in him was the life of men and the light of men'" (Dallin H. Oaks, "The Light and Life of the World," *Ensign*, Nov. 1987, 63).

"There is no greater expression of love than the heroic Atonement performed by the Son of God. Were it not for the plan of our Heavenly Father, established before the world began, in a very real sense, all mankind—past, present, and future—would have been left without the hope of eternal progression" (M. Russell Ballard, "The Atonement and the Value of One Soul," *Ensign*, May 2004, 84).

"The Atonement and the Resurrection accomplish many things. The Atonement cleanses us of sin on condition of our repentance. Repentance is the condition on which mercy is extended. After all we can do to pay to the uttermost farthing and make right our wrongs, the Savior's grace is activated in our lives through the Atonement, which purifies us and can perfect us. Christ's Resurrection overcame death and gave us the assurance of life after death" (James E. Faust, "The Atonement: Our Greatest Hope," *Ensign*, Nov. 2001, 18).

NOTES:

AND WHAT IS IT THAT YE SHALL *hope* FOR?
BEHOLD I SAY UNTO YOU THAT YE SHALL HAVE HOPE
THROUGH THE ATONEMENT OF *Christ* AND THE POWER OF HIS
RESURRECTION, TO BE RAISED UNTO LIFE ETERNAL,
AND THIS BECAUSE OF YOUR FAITH IN HIM ACCORDING TO
THE PROMISE.

MORONI 7:41

AND WHAT IS IT THAT YE SHALL *hope* FOR?
BEHOLD I SAY UNTO YOU THAT YE SHALL HAVE HOPE
THROUGH THE ATONEMENT OF *Christ* AND THE POWER OF HIS
RESURRECTION, TO BE RAISED UNTO LIFE ETERNAL,
AND THIS BECAUSE OF YOUR FAITH IN HIM ACCORDING TO
THE PROMISE.

MORONI 7:41

LESSON FOUR

THE MIRACLE OF FORGIVENESS

Hymns

No. 172, "In Humility, Our Savior"
No. 185, "Reverently and Meekly Now"
No. 140, "Did You Think to Pray"

SUMMARY:

1. Repentance and forgiveness are crucial to our spiritual health. The miracle of forgiveness can bring peace, comfort, and hope into our lives. When we cast off sin, repent, and are forgiven, we can find rest in the Savior. Without these two marvelous gifts, we could not return to our Heavenly Father. All men need repentance; repentance is necessary for serious sins as well as small sins against God. We must make repentance part of our everyday lives. Through sincere, continued repentance, we can unlock the miracle of God's forgiveness which brings us peace and comfort.

2. The repentance process is the same for each man; God does not play favorites, and each man must repent for his sins in the same way. First, a person must recognize the sin and experience godly sorrow. Feeling sorry for or regret over our sins isn't enough. Godly sorrow produces a change in heart, which is the first key to repentance. This change in heart should then prod the person repenting to action.

Abandoning sin is the next step of repentance. It is not merely enough to wish to change one's life or desire not to sin again. In order to truly repent, we must forsake the sin and avoid it with all our efforts. This means avoiding places, people, attitudes, and other things that could stir up memories of the sin and cause us to transgress again. Often, in cases of serious transgression, confession to proper church authorities is necessary. This confession must be voluntary and ensures that the proper controls are set in place so the transgressor can obtain forgiveness. This confession also lifts and helps carry the burden of sin so the transgressor can begin to feel peace again. Another step of repentance is restitution. The truly humbled will do everything in his or her power to not only forsake the sin but also to set right what he or she has wronged. We must restore everything to the best of our abilities. We are able to complete the repentance process when we free ourselves from hate and bitterness and make restitution where we can.

3. We cannot complete the repentance process without a rededication of our lives to the Lord. Our hearts can't be completely humble and penitent when we repent but do not attend our meetings, pay our tithing, magnify our callings, and try our best to live as the Lord would have us live them. Complete repentance includes surrendering our will to the Lord and submitting ourselves to him. This means we will take up his cause and keep the commandments.

QUOTES:

"Sometimes a guilt consciousness overpowers a person with such a heaviness that when a repentant one looks back and sees the ugliness, the loathsomeness of the transgression, he is almost overwhelmed and wonders, 'Can the Lord ever forgive me? Can I ever forgive myself?' But when one reaches the depths of despondency and feels the hopelessness of his position, and when he cries out to God for mercy in helplessness but in faith, there comes a still, small, but penetrating voice whispering to his soul, 'Thy sins are forgiven thee'" (Spencer W. Kimball, "God Will Forgive," *Ensign*, Mar. 1982, 2).

As we struggle toward that perfection which Jesus Christ holds out for us, let us give emphasis to forgiveness. Let us cultivate that aspect of our character and rejoice in the spirit of forgiveness, which is the comforting message of the Atonement" (Theodore M. Burton, "To Forgive Is Divine," *Ensign*, May 1983, 70).

"If there is discipline required for a serious transgression against you, leave that to the Church and civil authorities. Don't burden your own life with thoughts of retribution. The Lord's mill of justice grinds slowly, but it grinds exceedingly well. In the Lord's economy, no one will escape the consequences of unresolved violation of His laws. In His time and in His way full payment will be required for unrepented evil acts" (Richard G. Scott, "Peace of Conscience and Peace of Mind," *Ensign*, Nov. 2004, 15).

NOTES:

If you have ignored warnings and your life has been damaged or disabled by a rough road, there is help available. Through that help you can renew and rebuild your damaged life. You can start over again and change your course from a downward, twisting, disappointing path to a superhighway to peace and happiness.

— Richard G. Scott, "Finding Forgiveness," *Ensign*, May 1995.

If you have ignored warnings and your life has been damaged or disabled by a rough road, there is help available. Through that help you can renew and rebuild your damaged life. You can start over again and change your course from a downward, twisting, disappointing path to a superhighway to peace and happiness.

— Richard G. Scott, "Finding Forgiveness," *Ensign*, May 1995.

If you have ignored warnings and your life has been damaged or disabled by a rough road, there is help available. Through that help you can renew and rebuild your damaged life. You can start over again and change your course from a downward, twisting, disappointing path to a superhighway to peace and happiness.

— Richard G. Scott, "Finding Forgiveness," *Ensign*, May 1995.

If you have ignored warnings and your life has been damaged or disabled by a rough road, there is help available. Through that help you can renew and rebuild your damaged life. You can start over again and change your course from a downward, twisting, disappointing path to a superhighway to peace and happiness.

— Richard G. Scott, "Finding Forgiveness," *Ensign*, May 1995.

If you have ignored warnings and your life has been damaged or disabled by a rough road, there is help available. Through that help you can renew and rebuild your damaged life. You can start over again and change your course from a downward, twisting, disappointing path to a superhighway to peace and happiness.

— Richard G. Scott, "Finding Forgiveness," *Ensign*, May 1995.

PRAYER, THE PASSPORT TO SPIRITUAL POWER

Hymns

No. 144, "Secret Prayer"
No. 142, "Sweet Hour of Prayer"
No. 123, "Oh, May My Soul Commune with Thee"

SUMMARY:

1. We are required to pray to our Heavenly Father; this is not optional. We are not encouraged to pray or be reminded that we should pray; we are commanded to pray just as we are commanded to pay our tithing or to keep the Sabbath day holy. Sincere, constant prayer generally allows us to feel the love of the Lord and gives us the guidance of the Holy Ghost; therefore, we are better able to resist temptation and sin, and we are more able to keep the commandments. We should express gratitude in our prayers, pray for our leaders and missionaries, and we should pray for the Lord's help in our lives and in the lives of our loved ones. Praying is a privilege. When we sincerely pray with real intent, we can clearly communicate with God and feel of His love for us.

2. Our personal prayers should be private and vocal. When we can pray without insecurities or pretense, we are able to openly communicate with God. This real, open communication allows us to express our hopes and desires and gives us the opportunity to hear direction and guidance from the Lord. We should not hold back in our personal

prayers, but instead, we should open up and be honest with our Lord. He knows are hearts already, even if we do not open up in prayer.

We should pray in our families every morning and night and each family member should have the opportunity to pray. Our example and attitudes on prayer teach our children the importance of prayer. We must remember to teach our children that family prayer is neither a routine nor a chore. Also, we should remember that when we pray in a group setting, even in our families, our prayers must be appropriate for the occasion. Our purpose in prayer is to communicate with our Father in Heaven, and we need to be mindful of that. Family prayers, invocations, blessings on the food, and dedicatory prayers are all different, and we should tailor our prayers to fit the circumstances.

3. Prayer is real communication with our Heavenly Father, and communication requires two parties. We must not forget to listen for several minutes after we pray. The Lord hears all our prayers, and when we feel He is not answering them, we need to re-evaluate how well we are listening for answers. If our prayers have been sincere, we will receive a feeling of warmth and spiritual calmness that testifies that our prayers have been heard. In addition, we must remember to heed the advice and guidance we receive from prayer. Prayer is a privilege, and we cannot disregard the guidance and blessings we receive from prayer. When we pray sincerely, we will truly feel our Father in Heaven's love, and we will know that he does hear and answer our prayers.

QUOTES:

"God is with this people. But we are required to hearken to His voice, obey His commandments, and humble ourselves before Him. . . . There is a calmness prevailing among the Mormons—so called—that is a marvel and a wonder to the world. . . . The reason of our calmness is—God is our friend, our lawgiver, our deliverer. If the Lord cannot sustain His work, we certainly cannot. But He can. He has always done it, and will do it to the end. Therefore I say to the Saints, fear not. Trust in God. Let not your hearts be faint. Let your prayers ascend to the ears of the Lord of Sabbath day and night. Ask what you want. When you do that, the Lord will answer your prayers, if you ask what is right. There is where our strength lies. It is in God" (Wilford Woodruff, in *Teachings of Presidents of the Church: Wilford Woodruff* 2004, 106).

"When we remember that each of us is literally a spirit son or daughter of God, we will not find it difficult to approach our Heavenly Father in prayer" (Thomas S. Monson, "Your Eternal Home," *Ensign*, May 2000, 52).

"The special language of prayer follows different forms in different languages, but the principle is always the same. We should address prayers to our Heavenly Father in words which speakers of that language associate with love and respect and reverence and closeness" (Dallin H. Oaks, "The Language of Prayer," *Ensign*, May 1993, 15).

NOTES:

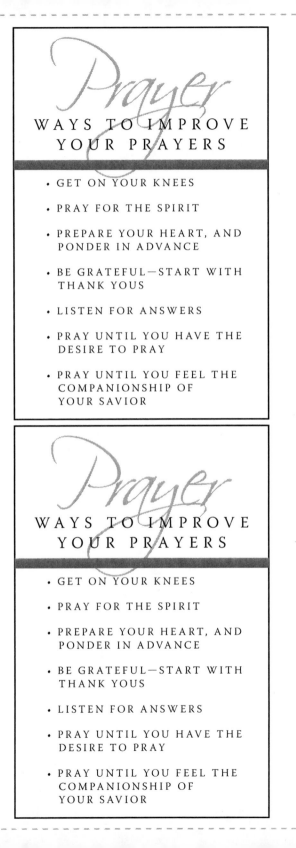

Prayer

WAYS TO IMPROVE
YOUR PRAYERS

- GET ON YOUR KNEES

- PRAY FOR THE SPIRIT

- PREPARE YOUR HEART, AND
  PONDER IN ADVANCE

- BE GRATEFUL—START WITH
  THANK YOUS

- LISTEN FOR ANSWERS

- PRAY UNTIL YOU HAVE THE
  DESIRE TO PRAY

- PRAY UNTIL YOU FEEL THE
  COMPANIONSHIP OF
  YOUR SAVIOR

Prayer

WAYS TO IMPROVE
YOUR PRAYERS

- GET ON YOUR KNEES

- PRAY FOR THE SPIRIT

- PREPARE YOUR HEART, AND
  PONDER IN ADVANCE

- BE GRATEFUL—START WITH
  THANK YOUS

- LISTEN FOR ANSWERS

- PRAY UNTIL YOU HAVE THE
  DESIRE TO PRAY

- PRAY UNTIL YOU FEEL THE
  COMPANIONSHIP OF
  YOUR SAVIOR

LESSON SIX

DISCOVERING
THE SCRIPTURES FOR
OURSELVES

Hymns

No. 277, "*As I Search the Holy Scriptures*"
No. 274, "*The Iron Rod*"
No. 85, "*How Firm a Foundation*"

SUMMARY:

1. As members of the Church, we often get into the habit of forgetting what a blessing the scriptures are. We are privileged to live in a time when the word of God is readily accessible; it was not that long ago that the world did not have access to the scriptures. Not only do we need to read the scriptures, but we must also make them precious to us and study them. Often, we may feel we know quite a bit about the scriptures, but really, we have only scratched the surface. The scriptures are meant to be studied over and over again; we must not stop. Studying the scriptures helps us more fully commit to the Lord. Our scriptures contain the fullness of the gospel and they outline more completely the ways in which we must serve the Lord and follow His commandments. True study of the scriptures calls for application of the principles contained within.

2. Learning by example is one of the most effective teaching and learning methods. When we study the stories in the scriptures, the consequences and outcomes of righteousness and wickedness are

plainer for us to understand, and we are more able to apply them to situations we face daily. All the strengths and weaknesses of men have been outlines in the scriptures. From pride and contention to motivation, loyalty, and humility, the scriptures teach proper spiritual living. These teachings and this knowledge is available to all who ponder and study the scriptures. Furthermore, we need to become both hearers and doers of the word of God. To become hearers, we have to diligently study the scriptures. To become doers, we must take the knowledge we have gained from our study and act upon it.

3. Those trying to find God in their lives need not look further. The scriptures contain an account of all that God has revealed to men through His servants. We may not be able to walk with God on this earth, but we can learn about and establish a relationship with Him and Jesus Christ through the scriptures. As we read the scriptures, we draw closer to God and learn to love Him more. When we have more love for Him and His Son, Jesus Christ, we find it easier to follow His commandments and return to Him.

QUOTES:

"Through my scripture reading and the prayers that accompany my study, I have gained knowledge which brings me peace and helps me keep my energies focused on eternal priorities. Because I started reading the scriptures daily, I have learned about my Heavenly Father, His Son Jesus Christ, and what I need to do to be like Them. I have learned about the Holy Ghost and how to qualify for His companionship. I have learned about my identity as a daughter of God. Essentially, I have learned who I am, why I am here on earth, and what I should be doing with my life" (Julie B. Beck, "My Soul Delighteth in the Scriptures," *Ensign*, May 2004, 107).

"Reading habits vary widely. There are rapid readers and slow readers, some who read only small snatches at a time and others who persist without stopping until the book is finished. Those who delve into the scriptural library, however, find that to understand requires more than casual reading or perusal—there must be concentrated study. It is certain that one who studies the scriptures every day accomplishes far more than one who devotes considerable time one day and then lets days go by before continuing. Not only should we study each day, but there should be a regular time set aside when we can concentrate without interference" (Howard W. Hunter, "Reading the Scriptures," *Ensign*, Nov. 1979, 64).

"We should make daily study of the scriptures a lifetime pursuit. . . . One of the most important things you can do . . . is to immerse yourselves in the scriptures. Search them diligently. . . . Learn the doctrine. Master the principles. . . . You must . . . see that studying and searching the scriptures is not a burden laid upon [us] by the Lord, but a marvelous blessing and opportunity" (Ezra Taft Benson, "Godly Characteristics of the Master," *Ensign*, Nov. 1986, 47).

NOTES: _____

5 Ways to Make Scripture Study More Meaningful

- Set aside time each day to focus on your reading
- Begin and end with prayer
- Keep a notebook handy to jot down impressions and guidance
- Use a dictionary or other reference to help you understand words you do not know
- Share your feelings and testimony with a spouse or a loved one

5 Ways to Make Scripture Study More Meaningful

- Set aside time each day to focus on your reading
- Begin and end with prayer
- Keep a notebook handy to jot down impressions and guidance
- Use a dictionary or other reference to help you understand words you do not know
- Share your feelings and testimony with a spouse or a loved one

5 Ways to Make Scripture Study More Meaningful

- Set aside time each day to focus on your reading
- Begin and end with prayer
- Keep a notebook handy to jot down impressions and guidance
- Use a dictionary or other reference to help you understand words you do not know
- Share your feelings and testimony with a spouse or a loved one

LESSON SEVEN

PERSONAL
TESTIMONY

Hymns

No. 137, "Testimony"
No. 136, "I Know that My Redeemer Lives"
No. 135, "My Redeemer Lives"

SUMMARY:

1. Each person can receive a testimony of the truthfulness of the gospel. A testimony cannot be gained through books, teachers, or other education. Instead, a testimony is a revelation that comes directly from Heavenly Father through the Holy Ghost. Not only do we need to study and gain spiritual knowledge to receive this witness, but we must also fast and pray and align our hearts with the Spirit. There is a difference between knowing and feeling, and when we know of the truthfulness of the gospel, we have received revelation. A testimony can only be understood and explained through the Spirit which communicates in the language of the heart. Obtaining a testimony opens opportunities of great joy and reward.

2. Now that we understand that each person can have a testimony, we must learn the necessary steps to obtain that testimony. The proper procedure to gain a testimony is study, think, pray, do. These steps prepare and humble our spirits to receive a testimony. The Lord

is not the person holding us back from obtaining this knowledge. We hold ourselves back; the Lord is eager to give us the knowledge of the gospel. However, we cannot be lazy and careless with such a precious gift. A testimony requires us to strive and prepare to receive it, and a testimony requires that we continue to strengthen and increase that testimony. If we do not sharpen our testimonies, they weaken. We must pray continually to keep the Spirit with us so our testimonies can grow.

3. Gaining a testimony takes study and prayer as well as application. Losing a testimony is effortless. We must fight all the time to keep our testimonies, and the best way to fight for our testimonies is to bear them. When we have the Spirit with us, testimony meetings become opportunities for us to be enriched and enlightened; we cannot cheat ourselves by not participating in these special meetings. However, we should keep in mind a few guidelines when we participate in a testimony meeting. First, we should remember that regardless of how often these words are said, the most powerful words are "I know." Second, we need to remember that testimony meetings are not opportunities to gives sermons or travelogues. Finally, we should keep in mind the best thing to do is to say how we feel. When we stick to our testimonies, the Spirit carries the message to those listening; we need not say more than that.

QUOTES:

"Your testimony of Jesus Christ is the most important anchor that you can have to help hold you, steadfast and immovable, to principles of righteousness" (Elder M. Russell Ballard, "Speaking Today: Steadfast in Christ," *Ensign*, Dec. 1993, 52).

"Our testimony comes by the gift and power of the Holy Ghost. The testimony received and carried within us enables us to hold a steady course in times of prosperity and to overcome doubt and fear in times of adversity. Each of us needs to know what a testimony is, how we can get it, and what our responsibilities are once we have received a testimony" (Robert D. Hales, "The Importance of Receiving a Personal Testimony," *Ensign*, Nov. 1994, 20).

"A testimony of the truth of the gospel does not come the same way to all people. Some receive it in a unique, life-changing experience. Others gain a testimony slowly, almost imperceptibly until, one day, they simply know" (Joseph B. Wirthlin, "Pure Testimony," *Ensign*, Nov. 2000, 22).

NOTES:

My Testimony

LESSON EIGHT

SELFLESS SERVICE

Hymns

No. 270, "I'll Go Where You Want Me to Go"
No. 243, "Let Us All Press On"
No. 220, "Lord, I Would Follow Thee"

SUMMARY:

1. The Savior is our best example of service to others. The better we understand His life and ministry, the better able we are to serve those around us. The Lord is mindful of our needs and the needs of others. Often, He meets these needs through acts of service. As members of the Church, we must recognize that we need to support and strengthen each other through service, regardless of our calling, position, or standing in the Church. Sometimes it becomes easy for us to fall into a routine of just paying our tithing, praying once daily, attending our meetings, and only doing what is required of us. However, we can't forget that we are also required to serve others and that we have been given talents and abilities to serve.

2. Not only do we need to serve others, we must also teach our youth to serve. Teaching our youth to serve and to look for opportunities to serve will help safeguard them against inactivity in the Church. Young men should learn to recognize the gospel working in the

lives of others and must learn early to practice the principle of home teaching. Young women of the Church should likewise be encouraged to engage in quiet acts of service.

3. Serving others gives our lives more meaning. We can trust the Savior when He said that by losing ourselves in service for Him, we find ourselves; when we focus on the needs of others, we forget to focus on ourselves. Not only are our lives enriched, but also, through service, we draw closer to the Lord, which fills our lives with joy. Regarding service, quite a contrast can be seen between the ways of the Lord and the ways of the world. As conditions in the world becomes more and more wicked, Church members will we severely tried. We can fight trials and progress spiritually by frequent, sincere service to others. True happiness can come when we forget our self-interests and lose ourselves in service.

QUOTES:

"Selfless service projects are the projects of the gospel. They have continuity. They are not one-time special events based on entertainment and fun and games. They need not be regimented nor regulated. Selfless service projects are people-to-people projects. They are face-to-face, eye-to-eye, voice-to-ear, heart-to-heart, spirit-to-spirit, and hand-in-hand, people-to-people projects" (William R. Bradford, "Selfless Service," *Ensign*, Nov. 1987, 75)

"Service changes people. It refines, purifies, gives a finer perspective, and brings out the best in each one of us. It gets us looking outward instead of inward. It prompts us to consider others' needs ahead of our own. Righteous service is the expression of true charity, such as the Savior showed" (Derek A. Cuthbert, "The Spirituality of Service," *Ensign*, May 1990, 12).

"Fathers and mothers, with your strength of example you will influence your sons and daughters for eternity with examples of loving, uncomplaining service far more convincingly by *doing* than only by saying. Show your children a life of love for them by a life of love and service to the Church and to our Father's children in spiritual need" (Russell C. Taylor, "The Joy of Service," *Ensign*, Nov. 1984, 23).

NOTES:

Joy in Service!

MY THREE SERVICE GOALS

Service Act: _____

_____

Description: _____

_____

_____

Goal Date: _____

Service Act: _____

_____

Description: _____

_____

_____

Goal Date: _____

Service Act: _____

_____

Description: _____

_____

_____

Goal Date: _____

LESSON NINE

FORGIVING OTHERS WITH ALL OUR HEARTS

Hymns

No. 131, "More Holiness Give Me"
No. 140, "Did You Think to Pray"
No. 308, "Love One Another"

SUMMARY:

1. In order to gain eternal life, we must be forgiven of our sins. One of the best things we can do to help secure that forgiveness is to forgive others. True forgiveness is sincere and heartfelt and includes forgetting. Just as we want the Lord to forgive and then forget our sins, we too must also forgive and forget. We need to forgive with all our hearts in order to stand worthy before God. Words of forgiveness alone do not satisfy the Lord's requirements. Our hearts need to be cleansed of all bitterness and malice, spite and vengeance before we can say we have truly forgiven our brethren.

2. Forgiveness is not necessarily easy. Often, not only do we not forgive others, but we also pass judgment on them. It is not our place to judge others. The Lord has said that all that is required of us is to forgive our brethren, and He will take care of the rest. We need to be reminded that the Lord will judge us with the same measures we judge others. We need to show mercy to others in order to have mercy shown unto us. Part of mercy is forgiveness,

no matter how difficult it may seem. We can forgive others, but this takes willingness on our part to let go of harsh feelings and allow peace into our hearts. Many believe that forgiveness is only a characteristic of the divine, yet it is required of us. The Lord never requires something that cannot be accomplished. We can learn to forgive if we turn to Him for help and guidance.

3. Forgiveness brings with it many blessings. When we are offended, we often hold bitterness and hatred in our hearts toward the offender, thinking that these feelings will injure the offender like we have been injured. However, holding these feelings in our hearts only damages our own spirits. This is especially true in a situation where a person isn't even aware he or she has offended us. For this reason, the Lord requires us to forgive even if the other party has not taken steps to establish peace. Without forgiveness, we cannot have this peace in our hearts, homes, or wards. There will always be occasions when feelings are hurt and words and actions misunderstood. When we remain close to the Spirit, we can overcome feelings of bitterness and avarice and feel the Lord's peace.

QUOTES:

"How difficult it is for any of us to forgive those who have injured us. We are all prone to brood on the evil done us. That brooding becomes as a gnawing and destructive canker. Is there a virtue more in need of application in our time than the virtue of forgiving and forgetting?" (Gordon B. Hinckley, "Of You It Is Required to Forgive," *Ensign*, June 1991, 2).

"I wish today to speak of forgiveness. I think it may be the greatest virtue on earth, and certainly the most needed. There is so much of meanness and abuse, of intolerance and hatred. There is so great a need for repentance and forgiveness. It is the great principle emphasized in all of scripture, both ancient and modern" (Gordon B. Hinckley,

"Forgiveness," *Ensign*, Nov. 2005, 81).

"Those who wish to consider themselves as disciples of the Master must understand that we, like the first servant, owe a great debt to our Heavenly King for the many gifts we have received from Him. This understanding unlocks the door to the gifts of repentance and our own forgiveness. The retention of these gifts depends upon our faithful forgiveness of those who have offended us. The Savior said, 'Blessed are the merciful: for they shall obtain mercy' (Matt. 5:7) and 'With what judgment ye judge, ye shall be judged' (Matt. 7:2)" (Cecil O. Samuelson, Jr., "Words of Jesus: Forgiveness," *Ensign*, Feb. 2003, 48).

NOTES:

I, THE LORD, WILL
FORGIVE
WHOM I WILL
FORGIVE,
BUT OF YOU
IT IS REQUIRED TO
FORGIVE
ALL MEN.
—D&C 64:10

I, THE LORD, WILL
FORGIVE
WHOM I WILL
FORGIVE,
BUT OF YOU
IT IS REQUIRED TO
FORGIVE
ALL MEN.
—D&C 64:10

I, THE LORD, WILL
FORGIVE
WHOM I WILL
FORGIVE,
BUT OF YOU
IT IS REQUIRED TO
FORGIVE
ALL MEN.
—D&C 64:10

I, THE LORD, WILL
FORGIVE
WHOM I WILL
FORGIVE,
BUT OF YOU
IT IS REQUIRED TO
FORGIVE
ALL MEN.
—D&C 64:10

I, THE LORD, WILL
FORGIVE
WHOM I WILL
FORGIVE,
BUT OF YOU
IT IS REQUIRED TO
FORGIVE
ALL MEN.
—D&C 64:10

LESSON TEN

FORTIFYING OURSELVES AGAINST EVIL INFLUENCES

Hymns

No. 106, "God Speed the Right"
No. 246, "Onward, Christian Soldiers"
No. 250, "We Are All Enlisted"

SUMMARY:

1. Our world today has taken the attitude that God doesn't exist. Furthermore, the idea that Satan is also a myth is just as strong, if not stronger. Nothing could be further from the truth. The adversary is real and is waiting to deceive even the most righteous. All our attempts to resist him only give him more knowledge on how to subdue us. The adversary knows he cannot persuade righteous people to immediately jump into sin, so he leads them little by little. The one and only way to resist these influences is to call on the Creator himself for help. The Lord will never forcibly pull us away from sin, but He will inspire us to righteous acts through the Spirit. Those who yield to the promptings of the Spirit are guaranteed protection.

2. As said before, it is rare that Satan can influence the pure in heart to dive into deep sin. Instead, he uses flattery, lyings, cheatings, and deceivings to get the righteous to commit small sins first before tempting them with serious sin. It is much easier to protect

our souls rather than to fight for them once they have been taken. We can protect them by making righteous decisions about sin before we are faced with the sin itself. Now is not just the time to decide that we do not participate in specific sins. Instead, now is the time to decide that we will do whatever if takes to return to our Heavenly Father. This decision ensures that we will avoid the destructive behavior of sin. We place ourselves in vulnerable positions when we are indecisive and discouraged. We must decide now to follow the example of the Savior and reject Satan.

3. Satan knows our weaknesses and is more likely to attack us in those weak places. Where he has succeeded once, he will try again, unless we fortify ourselves and turn those weaknesses to strengths. We will fall again just like we did the first time. We must be honest with ourselves and the Lord about our weaknesses and our sins; they are our responsibility. When we acknowledge that, we can then turn to the Lord for His divine help and guidance. Our course in overcoming Satan should draw us closer to the Lord and help us to have greater faith in Him, repent, and build the kingdom.

QUOTES:

"The Book of Mormon can help fortify all followers of Christ against the evil strategies of the devil. I add my witness to that of the Prophet Joseph Smith: 'The Book of Mormon [is] the most correct of any book on earth, and the keystone of our religion, and a man [will] get nearer to God by abiding by its precepts, than by any other book' (History of the Church, 4:461). The devil will have very little power over those who study and follow the precepts of this volume of scripture, and they will be well established on the road to eternal life" (Robert F. Orton, "Resisting Evil," *Ensign*, Aug. 2006, 24).

"I emphasize that fasting and prayer are great ways to receive the moral strength and spiritual strength to resist the temptations of Satan.

But you may say this is hard and unpleasant. I commend to you the example of the Savior. He went into the desert, where he fasted and prayed to prepare himself spiritually for his ministry. His temptation by the devil was great, but through the purification of his spirit he was able to triumph over all evil" (James E. Faust, "Serving the Lord and Resisting the Devil," *Liahona*, Nov. 1995, 3).

"The more obedient you are, the more you stand for true principles, the more the Lord can help you overcome temptation" (Richard G. Scott, "Making the Right Choices," *Ensign*, Nov. 1994, 37).

NOTES:

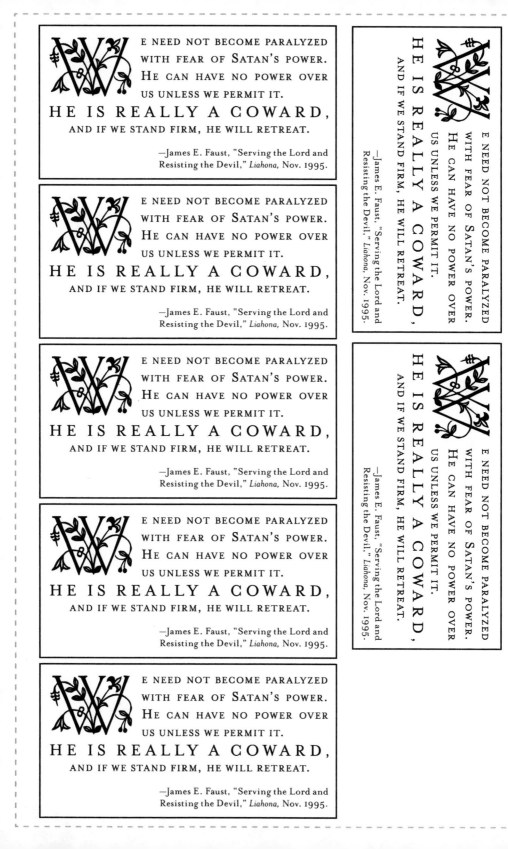

WE NEED NOT BECOME PARALYZED WITH FEAR OF SATAN'S POWER. HE CAN HAVE NO POWER OVER US UNLESS WE PERMIT IT.

HE IS REALLY A COWARD, AND IF WE STAND FIRM, HE WILL RETREAT.

—James E. Faust, "Serving the Lord and Resisting the Devil," *Liahona*, Nov. 1995.

PROVIDENT LIVING: APPLYING THE PRINCIPLES OF SELF-RELIANCE AND PREPARATION

Hymns

No. 226, *"Improve the Shining Moments"*
No. 252, *"Put Your Shoulder to the Wheel"*
No. 94, *"Come, Ye Thankful People"*

SUMMARY:

1. As members of the Church, we are commanded to be self-reliant and independent. We are responsible for our own physical, economical, spiritual, and emotional well-being. No member of the Church should place the burden of caring for the well-being of his family to another when he is capable of taking care of them. We have been called on to be personally prepared and to have our families prepared as well. We should take this counsel as seriously and with as much purpose as we do any other direction from the Lord.

2. Part of this preparedness includes food storage and emergency preparation. We have been counseled to acquire at least a year's supply of bare necessities to sustain our families. In addition, we can prepare ourselves for emergencies by keeping a garden. Furthermore, we should keep a savings account. We should practice provident living, which includes managing our resources wisely. We should also work. Work brings accomplishments,

achievement, and self-esteem. We are commanded to work and to do our part in assisting our families even if we require some help in supporting them. Everyone who needs assistance can do something to help. Work helps us feel productive and responsible, and we should work and teach our children the value of work.

3. To properly follow the Lord's counsel to be self-reliant, we must live within our means, avoid debt, and save our money. We need to learn to live without and must take caution that our wants don't turn into needs. Furthermore, we should set some of our income aside for emergencies, and we need to teach our children to do the same. This saving and preparing is not a one-time event; rather, it is a way of life. Preparedness shouldn't be sought after solely for emergencies and disasters. Instead, we should prepare to live wisely each day as the Lord has counseled us to. This lifestyle blesses us each day and fortifies us for the days to come.

QUOTES:

"Many programs have been set up by well-meaning individuals to aid those who are in need. However, many of these programs are designed with the shortsighted objective of 'helping people,' as opposed to 'helping people help themselves.' Our efforts must always be directed toward making able-bodied people self-reliant" (Marion G. Romney, "The Celestial Nature of Self-Reliance," *Ensign*, June 1984, 3).

"President Kimball's complete dedication to his work sets a high standard for all of us. We have a moral obligation to exercise our personal capabilities of mind, muscle, and spirit in a way that will return to the Lord, our families, and our society the fruits of our best efforts. To do less is to live our lives unfulfilled. It is to deny ourselves and those dependent upon us opportunity and advantage. We work to earn a living, it is true; but as we toil, let us also remember that we are building a life. Our work determines what that life will be" (J. Richard Clarke,

"The Value of Work," *Ensign*, May 1982, 77).

"Unfortunately, there has been fostered in the minds of some an expectation that when we experience hard times, when we have been unwise and extravagant with our resources and have lived beyond our means, we should look to either the Church or government to bail us out. Forgotten by some of our members is an underlying principle of the Church welfare plan that 'no true Latter-day Saint will, while physically able, voluntarily shift from himself the burden of his own support' (Marion G. Romney, in Conference Report, Oct. 1973, 106)" (Ezra Taft Benson, "Prepare for the Days of Tribulation," *Ensign*, Nov. 1980, 32).

NOTES:

NOW IS THE TIME

STARTING POINTS FOR BECOMING PREPARED

- Obtain informational pamphlets on dealing with disasters from your local fire department or Red Cross. Review these with your family and organize an action plan for a variety of disasters.

- Keep a flashlight with fresh batteries near your bed.

- Help coordinate and rotate your family's food storage. Make sure necessary items are well stocked.

- Learn the signals your community uses to warn of potential disasters. Know where to tune your radio for instructions when the signals are given.

- Assemble a first-aid kit and learn how to use it properly.

- Know basic fire safety rules, including how to extinguish fires and avoid smoke.

- Make a priority list of items to bring with you if you need to leave home in a hurry. Necessities and things that can't easily be replaced, such as photos and scrapbooks, should come first. Remember, however, that you and your family are more important than any objects.

- If you hear of a disaster elsewhere, ask yourself, "What would I have done in that situation?"

Darrin Lythgoe, "Idea List: Are You Prepared?" *New Era*, Mar. 2000.

MORE PREPAREDNESS IDEAS AND GOALS

_____

_____

_____

_____

_____

_____

_____

_____

LESSON TWELVE

INTEGRITY

Hymns

No. 239, *"Choose the Right"*
No. 254, *"True to the Faith"*
No. 237, *"Do What Is Right"*

SUMMARY:

1. Integrity is part of a good character and is essential in returning to our Father in Heaven. It is the capability of a person to live by his beliefs and promises, coupled with a desire to do so. Integrity is a state of being whole, honest, pure, and genuine, and it is a priceless virtue. Having integrity means that a person disregards what others may think of him and instead measures himself against his own standards and against God's standards. Men with integrity are sure and steady rather than sorrowful and uncertain. As members of the Church, we should frequently take inventory of our lives to ensure that we are not hiding dishonesty, hypocrisy, or rationalizations. Integrity must be an integral part of our lives.

2. We can show our integrity by keeping our covenants. The covenants we make with the Lord are sacred, and we should not treat them lightly as the Lord does not treat them lightly. It is easy to justify and rationalize our behavior, but when we do, the Lord takes his Spirit from us.

When we covenant with the Lord, we often promise action in addition to avoidance of sin. When we make a covenant in the temple, for example, we pledge to do righteous works. To keep this covenant, we must honor our pledge to not only avoid wickedness and sin but also to take action; this covenant can be effortlessly broken by doing nothing.

Breaking our covenants or being dishonest can almost always be traced back to self-justification. Self-justification makes repentance impossible and cheats us out of peace, happiness, and the Spirit's companionship.

3. Our level of integrity directly influences our children's integrity. If we allow them or teach them to commit small acts of dishonesty, we are increasing their likelihood of committing larger acts of theft or dishonesty. We must teach our children that all sin, even small sin, is still sin. Members must teach their children that theft, dishonesty, cheating, and rationalization are acts that distance ourselves from the Lord and damage our integrity. We can teach them to have integrity through the many examples in the scriptures, which are full of stories about integrity. We can teach them the stories of Shadrach, Meshach, and Abednego or Daniel in the lion's den, who all honored their faith and commitment to the Lord in the face of adversity.

QUOTES:

"Our children should value honesty and integrity. They should know beforehand what their decisions will be when they are faced with crisis. They should know and understand that they are children of God, and that their eternal destiny is to so live that they will be worthy to return to his presence when they have completed their life's mission. Adults should not hinder their progress, but help them always to be true to their ideals and principles" (N. Eldon Tanner, "Integrity," *Ensign*, May 1977, 14).

"To me, integrity means always doing what is right and good, regardless of the immediate consequences. It means being righteous from the very depth of our soul, not only in our actions but, more importantly, in our thoughts and in our hearts. Personal integrity implies such trustworthiness and incorruptibility that we are incapable of being false to a trust or covenant" (Joseph B. Wirthlin, "Personal Integrity," *Ensign*, May 1990, 30).

"In our day, those found in dishonesty aren't put to death, but something within them dies. Conscience chokes, character withers, self-respect vanishes, and integrity dies. Without honesty, our lives disintegrate into ugliness, chaos, and a lack of any kind of security and confidence" (Gordon B. Hinckley, *Stand a Little Taller*, Eagle Gate, Salt Lake City, Utah, 2001, 178).

NOTES:

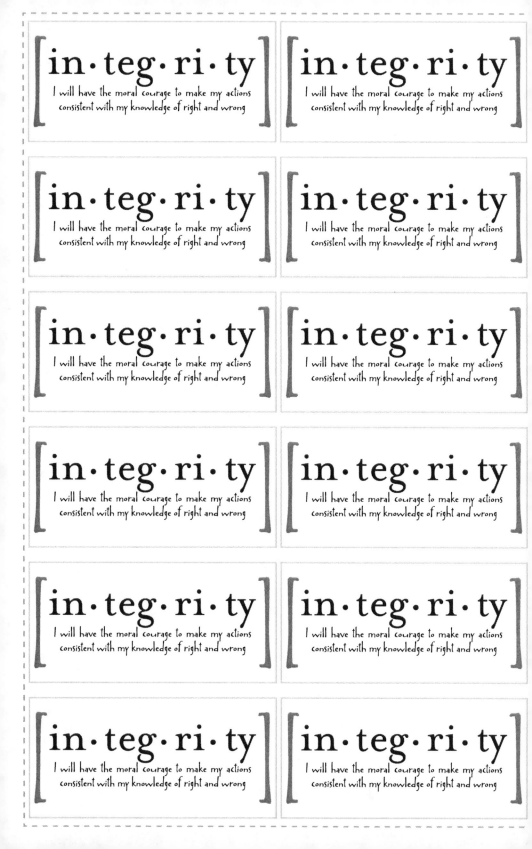

LESSON THIRTEEN

OBEDIENCE BORN OF
FAITH IN GOD

Hymns

No. 116, "Come, Follow Me"
No. 125, "How Gentle God's Commands"
No. 188, "Thy Will, O Lord, Be Done"

SUMMARY:

1. No Latter-day Saint will admit that it is easy to stay on the strait and narrow path. However, true faith in the Lord motivates us to stay on course. We need not understand all the principles in order to receive blessings and guidance; faith is sufficient to receive guidance and compel us to act on that guidance. Our faith does not allow us to idly stand by, but rather, it pushes us to discover and learn all we can in order to receive blessings from the Lord. Work must accompany our faith. Every member of the Church can be obedient to the commandments through faith and then action. Faith and works go hand in had. The more faith we have, the easier it is to be obedient, and the more obedient we are, the easier it becomes to have faith.

2. Willing, voluntary, happy obedience based on faith is not blind obedience. Obedience based on faith is true obedience to the Lord. This happens when we recognize God as our creator and that His commandments are righteous and for our good. In

addition, obedience based no faith is characterized by a desire to keep His commandments. Heavenly Father has proved Himself in everything. He loves us, watches out for us, guides us, and knows our limitations. Even when we do not fully understand the principles or purposes, obeying the Lord's commandments is never blind obedience.

3. The scriptures illustrate many examples of obedience through faith. Adam, Abraham, and Noah are all great examples of following the Lord's command without a full understanding. Each time they obeyed, they were blessed beyond measure. We too can receive these blessings if we have the faith to obey our Father's commands. Often, we want things reversed. We want the blessings manifest before we have faith to obey. However, the Lord knows our hearts and knows we must first have faith in Him. Being a righteous member of the Church takes immeasurable faith, but the blessings of peace, prosperity, and eternal life are priceless.

QUOTES:

"We cannot run our own way and have the blessing of God. Every one who attempts it will find he is mistaken. God will withdraw his Spirit from such, and they will be left to themselves to wander in the dark, and go down to perdition. It is expected of us that we shall move on a higher plane, that we shall feel that we are children of God, that God is our Father, and he will not be dishonored by disobedient children, or by those who fight against his laws and his priesthood. He expects us to live our religion, to obey His laws and keep His commandments" (John Taylor, in Teachings of Presidents of the Church: John Taylor [2001], 33).

"Latter-day Saints are not obedient because they are compelled to be obedient. They are obedient because they know certain spiritual truths and have decided, as an expression of their own individual agency, to obey the commandments of God. . . . We are not obedient because we are blind, we are obedient because we can see" (Boyd K. Packer "Agency and Control," *Ensign*, May 1983, 66).

"'Faith obedience' is a matter of trust. The question is simple: Do we trust our Heavenly Father? Do we trust our prophets?" (R. Conrad Schultz, "Faith Obedience," *Ensign*, May 2002, 29).

NOTES:

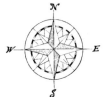

THERE IS NO NEED FOR YOU OR
ME IN THIS ENLIGHTENED AGE,
WHEN THE FULNESS OF THE
GOSPEL HAS BEEN RESTORED, TO
SAIL UNCHARTED SEAS OR TRAVEL
UNMARKED ROADS IN SEARCH
OF A "FOUNTAIN OF TRUTH." FOR
A LIVING HEAVENLY FATHER
HAS PLOTTED OUR COURSE AND
PROVIDED AN UNFAILING MAP—
OBEDIENCE.

—Thomas S. Monson, "Strength through Obedience,"
Ensign, July 1996.

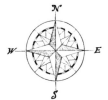

THERE IS NO NEED FOR YOU OR
ME IN THIS ENLIGHTENED AGE,
WHEN THE FULNESS OF THE
GOSPEL HAS BEEN RESTORED, TO
SAIL UNCHARTED SEAS OR TRAVEL
UNMARKED ROADS IN SEARCH
OF A "FOUNTAIN OF TRUTH." FOR
A LIVING HEAVENLY FATHER
HAS PLOTTED OUR COURSE AND
PROVIDED AN UNFAILING MAP—
OBEDIENCE.

—Thomas S. Monson, "Strength through Obedience,"
Ensign, July 1996.

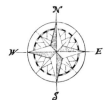

THERE IS NO NEED FOR YOU OR
ME IN THIS ENLIGHTENED AGE,
WHEN THE FULNESS OF THE
GOSPEL HAS BEEN RESTORED, TO
SAIL UNCHARTED SEAS OR TRAVEL
UNMARKED ROADS IN SEARCH
OF A "FOUNTAIN OF TRUTH." FOR
A LIVING HEAVENLY FATHER
HAS PLOTTED OUR COURSE AND
PROVIDED AN UNFAILING MAP—
OBEDIENCE.

—Thomas S. Monson, "Strength through Obedience,"
Ensign, July 1996.

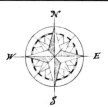

THERE IS NO NEED FOR YOU OR
ME IN THIS ENLIGHTENED AGE,
WHEN THE FULNESS OF THE
GOSPEL HAS BEEN RESTORED, TO
SAIL UNCHARTED SEAS OR TRAVEL
UNMARKED ROADS IN SEARCH
OF A "FOUNTAIN OF TRUTH." FOR
A LIVING HEAVENLY FATHER
HAS PLOTTED OUR COURSE AND
PROVIDED AN UNFAILING MAP—
OBEDIENCE.

—Thomas S. Monson, "Strength through Obedience,"
Ensign, July 1996.

LESSON FOURTEEN

"THOU SHALT HAVE NO OTHER GODS BEFORE ME"

Hymns

No. 66, "Rejoice, the Lord Is king"
No. 57, "We're Not Ashamed to Own Our Lord"
No. 72, "Praise to the Lord, the Almighty"

SUMMARY:

1. Placing our loyalty, our hearts, and our desires above God is worshipping false gods. Good men and women rarely deliberately reject God and His blessings. Instead, as we learn from the scriptures, men often turn to immediate and tangible things to trust in because faith in God is difficult and requires patience. Modern day false gods include material items such as clothes, cars, and homes, as well as power, prestige, or acknowledgement. We often forsake our God for sports, shopping, and vacations. Attachment to all these things makes us vulnerable to the adversary. Satan's grip on us can tighten very quickly if we do not let our grip on worldly things go and grasp the things of the Lord.

2. Righteous men and women are often prosperous. We learn in the Book of Mormon that each time the people were righteous, they prospered. Soon, that prosperity turned to a love of riches and luxury, and the people quickly fell into sin and wickedness as they forgot their God—the sole factor responsible for their prosperity.

We cannot be so naïve as to think that this lesson does not apply to us today. When the Lord blesses us with resources, we must remember that He expects us to use these resources to build up His kingdom. The riches and wealth we acquire from the Lord is not the problem. Instead, our attitude becomes the problem. When we recognize our prosperity and resources as a blessing from God, we will use them appropriately.

3. Shiny automobiles, wealth, jewelry, and power are not nearly as valuable as the blessings we receive from the Lord. However, we often have a hard time recognizing this principle. When we keep an eternal perspective, we are better able to see that celestial blessings from a God who has power over "worlds without number" (Moses 1:33) are priceless when compared to material items that profit us nothing in the kingdoms of heaven. Unfortunately, choosing not to worship idols is not enough. We must cast off our false gods and then actively worship our Heavenly Father. We must have faith in Him, repent, and spread the gospel to His children. We must leave the world behind and enter into the service of our God who has prepared our way for eternal life.

QUOTES:

"The term *idolatry* usually refers to the worship of a fetish, a graven image, or an imagined, unseen deity. But idolatry may exist on many levels: some create images to represent a deity, some idolize other humans, and some 'worship' material possessions or achievements. In essence, the practice of idolatry means putting worldly things ahead of God" (David H. Madsen, "No Other Gods before Me," *Ensign*, Jan. 1990, 48).

"Anything can become a 'golden calf.' When activities or material blessings become so important that by turning to them we turn from God, we are breaking the second commandment. We are walking 'in [our] own way, and after the image of [our] own god, whose image is in the likeness of the world, and whose substance is that of an idol, which waxeth old and shall perish' (D&C 1:16; emphasis added). The solution is to turn our affections back to God" (Dennis Largey, "Refusing to Worship Today's Graven Images," *Liahona*, Mar. 1998, 17).

"Sadly, many individuals don't know where to find God, and exclude Him from their lives. When spiritual needs arise, they may look to the left, the right, or round about. But looking to other people on the same level cannot satisfy spiritual shortages. When the immortal spirit is starved, hunger persists for something more filling" (Russell M. Nelson, "Thou Shalt Have No Other Gods," *Ensign*, May 1996, 14).

NOTES:

In What Ways Do We Allow Ourselves to Worship False Gods?

I asked some Latter-day Saints, "What is the modern application of the second commandment?" The following responses are a sample of those I received:

• "The scriptures say to have thoughts of God always within our hearts. Many people now fill their hearts with thoughts of riches, power, and fame. They worship their possessions, loving things without life."

• "We serve ourselves much too often when we should be serving the Lord. We must not worship our time—a graven image that takes the place of God in many cases. God asks us to sacrifice our time, making sure that he, not our own selfish interests, is first in our lives."

• "The graven images I see people worshiping are clothing, cars, homes, hobbies, and recreation. The fact that I spend more time deciding what to wear each morning than I do in prayer is very telling."

• "Alma 1:32 says, 'Those who did not belong to their church did indulge themselves in sorceries, and in idolatry or idleness.' This is something that I had never contemplated before: idleness as a form of idolatry."

• "Money is one of the most common images that people bow down to today. They bow down by giving up their integrity and honesty in dealing with others in order to obtain it. They bend their principles as they are bowing down."

• "Too often people make man their graven image. Because we are afraid of others' opinions, we won't serve others or be kind to those society looks down on. We worship others' praise and honor; we desire above all else the prestige others can give us. We want the right titles and awards. We want to wear the right clothing. We want to be popular."

—Dennis Largey, "Refusing to Worship Today's Graven Images," *Liahona*, Mar. 1998.

LESSON FIFTEEN

WE SHOULD BE A REVERENT PEOPLE

Hymns

No. 247, "We Love Thy House, O God"
No. 298, "Home Can Be a Heaven on Earth"
No. 113, "Our Savior's Love"

SUMMARY:

1. Reverence is not confined to Sunday worship, but should instead be a way of life and an attitude of devotion to God. Contrary to what we often teach our children, reverence is not just quiet whispers and folded arms in the chapel. Instead, reverence is characterized by happiness, holy devotion, respect, gratitude, and praise to the Lord. We can show reverence to the Lord and to Jesus Christ and their names in our daily lives. We are counseled not to profane the names of the Father or the Son and to avoid too frequent use of their names. However, it is not enough to avoid disrespectful use of the Lord's name. We must speak His name in holiness and reverence in our thoughts, discussions, and prayers. We should dedicate ourselves to a reverent and grateful attitude.

2. In addition to the reverent use of the Lord's name, we should also practice reverent use of the Lord's temples, chapel, and even our own homes. Like his gospel, the Lord's meetinghouses are simple; they are clean, and they are comfortable places where His children

can learn and worship without interference from too flashy and too ornate surroundings. We show reverence to our God when we can attend sacrament meetings in His chapels without being distracted by unrestrained children, noisy conversations, and social gatherings in the foyers. Respect is illustrated when we pick up after ourselves, arrive early for our meetings, and sing appropriate musical numbers. The Spirit will teach our hearts the best when we treat the Lord's meeting house for what it is: a place of reverent worship where Heavenly Father can dwell with us.

3. Developing reverence should begin in our homes, which should be extensions of our chapels and temples. In our homes, we should teach our children to pray and show respect for our Father in Heaven. In addition, our children must learn that not only are churches and temples places of reverence and learning, but also our homes are places of reverence and learning, and we must treat them accordingly. Family home evenings are great opportunities to help children invite the Spirit into our homes and recognize His presence through reverence. Furthermore, the home is a perfect place to practice good Sunday habits. Being prepared and spiritually ready to attend church should be emphasized. Also, we as parents should remember that not only our children but others also follow our lead in reverence. When we adopt a reverent lifestyle, rather than just on Sundays, we set a good example for those around us.

QUOTES:

"With our block-plan scheduling, three hours is a long time for a small child to sit in meetings. It is a long time for a mother who has small children around her. But with thoughtful training and careful consideration of all elements of the situation, a great improvement can be brought to pass. Mothers with small babies may plan to sit near the aisle so that, if necessary, they can leave quietly to care for their children"

(Gordon B. Hinckley, "Reverence and Morality," *Ensign*, May 1987, 45).

"Holy places have always been essential to the proper worship of God. For Latter-day Saints, such holy places include venues of historic significance, our homes, sacrament meetings, and temples. Much of what we reverence, and what we teach our children to reverence as holy and sacred, is reflected in these places. The faith and reverence associated with them and the respect we have for what transpires or has transpired in them make them holy. The importance of holy places and sacred space in our worship can hardly be overestimated" (Dennis B. Neuenschwander, "Holy Place, Sacred Space," *Ensign*, May 2003, 71).

"Reverence is the soul of true religion. Its seedbed is sincerity. Its quality is determined by the esteem in which one holds the object of his reverence as evidenced by his behavior toward that object. When that object is God, the genuinely reverent person has a worshipful adoration coupled with a respectful behavior toward him and all that pertains to him. The want of such appreciation or behavior smacks of irreverence" (Marion G. Romney, "Reverence," *Ensign*, Oct. 1976, 2)

NOTES:

Five Ways I Can Be a Better Example of Reverence

_____

_____

_____

_____

_____

Be still and know that I am God —Psalm 46:10

Five Ways I Can Be a Better Example of Reverence

_____

_____

_____

_____

_____

Be still and know that I am God —Psalm 46:10

LESSON SIXTEEN

THE SABBATH—A DELIGHT

Hymns

No. 280, "Welcome, Welcome, Sabbath Morning"
No. 64, "On This Day of Joy and Gladness"
No. 146, "Gently Raise the Sacred Strain"

SUMMARY:

1. From the time of Moses, the Lord has commanded His people to keep the Sabbath day holy; this has never been a suggestion or guideline. To many, breaking the Sabbath day is nothing. However, to the Lord, it is breaking a principle commandment. In our modern day, Sunday has become like any other day of the week; Sunday is for work, recreation, and occasionally for worship. We are counseled not to shop on Sundays and are told that shops would not need to be open if we, the buying public, did not patronize them on the Sabbath. Furthermore, we know that the Sabbath is not for hunting, sporting tournaments, shows, or other forms of entertainment. The Lord acknowledges that some must work on Sundays and that emergencies occur on the Sabbath. However, if we could have planned ahead and taken care of the situation before Sunday, we are still breaking the Sabbath.

2. Merely avoiding work and play on the Sabbath is not enough. The Sabbath day is set aside for spiritual learning and rest. First and foremost, the Sabbath is set aside for attending sacrament meeting. If we start our Sabbath day appropriately and attend our meetings with

a proper attitude, the Spirit we receive in those meetings will attend us for the rest of the day and influence our actions. The Sabbath day is a day to commune with the Lord, to study our scriptures, to fast, to confess our sins, to visit the sick and afflicted, to spread the gospel. However, all these things account for nothing if we do not attend our meetings and partake of the sacrament. We are required to partake of the sacrament. When we attend our meetings, we are blessed with the Spirit, we are able to participate in prayer, and we are able to be fellowshipped by other members. If we fail to attend our meetings, we miss out on these blessings regardless of our other pursuits. We go to meetings so we can worship our God.

3. The Lord gives us commandments for our benefit; therefore, it logically follows that the commandment to keep the Sabbath day holy is a blessing rather than a restriction on our freedom. We suffer when we break this commandment. In the end, we will not suffer for financial sacrifices to keep the Sabbath day holy. If we truly love the Lord, we will keep this simple commandment. When we set the Sabbath day aside for total devotion to and worship of our Lord, we convey to Him our sincere love and humility. As members of the Church, we often struggle with which activities are appropriate for Sunday. However, when we sincerely love the Lord and have His Spirit with us, we will know which Sunday activities are pleasing to Him and show Him respect and gratitude.

QUOTES:

"The injunction from God to 'Remember the sabbath day, to keep it holy' (Ex. 20:8) has been in force throughout human history. There is power in keeping the Sabbath day holy. I testify that God lives, that we are his children, that he loves us, and that he gives us commandments so he can bless us as we keep them and thereby have joy. As we keep the Sabbath day holy he will bless us, and we will achieve a quiet power for good as individuals, as families, and as nations, that we cannot obtain in any other way" (John H. Groberg, "The Power of Keeping the Sabbath Day Holy," *Ensign*, Nov. 1984, 79).

"Why has God asked us to honor the Sabbath day? The reasons I think are at least threefold. The first has to do with the physical need for rest and renewing. Obviously God, who created us, would know more than we do of the limits of our physical and nervous energy and strength. The second reason is, in my opinion, of far greater significance. It has to do with the need for regeneration and the strengthening of our spiritual being. God knows that, left completely to our own devices without regular reminders of our spiritual needs, many would degenerate into the preoccupation of satisfying earthly desires and appetites. This need for physical, mental, and spiritual regeneration is met in large measure by faithful observance of the Sabbath day" (James E. Faust, "The Lord's Day," *Ensign*, Nov. 1991, 33).

"Modern-day prophets have encouraged us not to shop on Sunday. . . . Those of us who shop on the Sabbath cannot escape responsibility for encouraging businesses to remain open on that day. Essential services must be provided, but most Sabbath transactions could be avoided if merchants and customers were determined to avoid doing business on the Lord's day" (Dallin H. Oaks, "Brother's Keeper," *Ensign*, Nov. 1986, 21).

NOTES:

WHAT IS THE SABBATH DAY?

1. It is a day of rest from our labors.

2. It is a holy day of worship.

3. It is a day to remember the Lord's atonement and resurrection.

4. It is a day to renew our baptismal covenants by partaking of the sacrament.

5. It is a day of prayer and fasting.

6. It is a day of finding uplift in music, hymns, and songs.

7. It is a day to prepare, meditate, and study the gospel.

8. It is a day to visit the sick and the afflicted, the widow and the orphan.

9. It is a day to strengthen our ties with our living families, do work for those who died without the ordinances of salvation, and write family histories.

10. It is a day for missionary preparation and work.

Charles Didier, "The Sabbath—Holy Day or Holiday?" *Ensign,* Oct. 1994.

WHAT IS THE SABBATH DAY?

1. It is a day of rest from our labors.

2. It is a holy day of worship.

3. It is a day to remember the Lord's atonement and resurrection.

4. It is a day to renew our baptismal covenants by partaking of the sacrament.

5. It is a day of prayer and fasting.

6. It is a day of finding uplift in music, hymns, and songs.

7. It is a day to prepare, meditate, and study the gospel.

8. It is a day to visit the sick and the afflicted, the widow and the orphan.

9. It is a day to strengthen our ties with our living families, do work for those who died without the ordinances of salvation, and write family histories.

10. It is a day for missionary preparation and work.

Charles Didier, "The Sabbath—Holy Day or Holiday?" *Ensign,* Oct. 1994.

LESSON SEVENTEEN

THE LAW OF CHASTITY

Hymns

No. 256, "As Zion's Youth in Latter Days"
No. 112, "Savior, Redeemer of my Soul"
No. 131, "More Holiness Give Me"

SUMMARY:

1. To the world, the Church's stand on chastity seems old fashioned; this long standing value is upheld not because it is an old tradition but because it is right. Complete chastity before marriage and complete fidelity after marriage brings happiness and joy into our lives. Any violation brings sorrow, emptiness, and pain. The Lord condemns and forbids all sexual practices outside of marriage. In addition, the Lord forbids all homosexual and acts of incest, period. Pure sex life within the proper bonds of marriage is approved. However, all sexual acts outside legalized marriage is abominable. It exploits others and is selfish, dishonest, and impure.

2. Men and women who participate in illicit acts and claim to do these acts in the name of love are being dishonest with themselves. Love includes respect and honor, and those involved cherish one another. Being selfish and disrespectful enough to participate in sexual acts outside of marriage isn't love, it is lust. Lust breeds hatred, loathing, and self-destruction. Often, we talk of love at first sight, but this is

merely a physical attraction, and to fall prey to physical urges based on this attraction is lust. Love, on the other hand, is wholesome and complete and includes much more than physical attraction. To keep our feelings of lust at bay, we should shun all forms of immorality, especially pornography. Pornography is garbage and is far too prevalent in our society. Nothing good comes from pornography. We should avoid all pornography and teach our children to avoid it like the plague. It is a cancer that spreads through and destroys families.

3. Children should be taught early to avoid immorality, and their parents should be their teachers. Parents should teach their children that upholding the law of chastity is not only expected by their earthly parents but also by their Heavenly Father and Jesus Christ. Do not allow your youth to become casual in their church attendance. Strong activity in the Church safeguards them against immoral acts. Teach modesty to your children. No excuse or reason warrants the exposure of their bodies. Furthermore, we should support and enforce the Church standards on dating. Dating and pairing off should be postponed until our children are sixteen years old. Finally, we as parents should be clean and use this example to teach our children to be clean and chaste.

QUOTES:

"Chastity and fidelity begin in the spirit, not in the body. They are an expression of the condition of our spirit. When our spirit is in tune with godly thinking and gospel truths, we want to live high standards, and our actions reflect that desire. Thus, chastity and fidelity are more than sexual abstinence before marriage and sexual fidelity after marriage. They express the quality of our spiritual life" (Terrance D. Olson, "Truths of Moral Purity," *Ensign*, Oct. 1998, 43).

"In matters of human intimacy, you must wait! You must wait until you can give everything, and you cannot give everything until you are legally and lawfully married. To give illicitly that which is not yours to give (remember, 'you are not your own') and to give only part of that which cannot be followed with the gift of your whole self is emotional Russian roulette. If you persist in pursuing physical satisfaction without the sanction of heaven, you run the terrible risk of such spiritual, psychic damage that you may undermine both your longing for physical intimacy and your ability to give wholehearted devotion to a later, truer love" (Jeffrey R. Holland, "Personal Purity," *Ensign*, Nov. 1998, 75).

"Immoral images from movies, television, magazines, and the Internet can put thoughts into our minds that compromise our happiness today and, if not repented of, for eternity" (Sheldon F. Child, "Words of Jesus: Chastity," *Ensign*, Jan. 2003, 44).

NOTES:

LESSON EIGHTEEN

HONORABLE, HAPPY, SUCCESSFUL MARRIAGE

Hymns

No. 300, "Families Can be Together Forever"
No. 308, "Love One Another"
No. 87, "God Is Love"

SUMMARY:

1. Honorable, eternal marriage ordained of God is essential to the plan of salvation. Only eternal marriage transcends death and lasts forever. The Lord set this standard with Adam and Eve and asked that we follow their example as part of His plan. The Lord's plan includes marriage and bearing children, and although the world considers a family a burden, we should strive for and look forward to an eternal family. Because eternal marriage is required for exaltation, the Lord will make provisions for those who have had no opportunity for an eternal companion; this will not be the case with those who abstain from marriage by choice.

2. Because eternal marriage transcends the grave, we should carefully prepare for our marriages. This planning includes fasting, prayer, pondering, and consulting with the Lord so that of all the decisions we make, the decision as to who shall be our eternal companion is correct and right. Couples approaching the commitment of eternal marriage must understand that marriage requires sacrifice,

compromise, worry, and a lifestyle change; marriage also brings sweet feelings and deep love and commitment. This love and happiness can be obtained if the couple decides to strive for a happy marriage. The formula for a good, strong marriage first involves a proper approach to marriage, which includes spouse selection. Secondly, each partner needs to be selfless and needs to focus on the good of the family rather than on the good of oneself. Third, each marriage should experience continued courtship and love. Finally, the couple must completely observe the Lord's commandments.

3. Two of the most important factors in the formula for a successful marriage are unselfishness and a strict observance of the commandments. A marriage is a partnership, and each person needs to reprioritize in order to obtain a happy marriage. The needs of the spouse must come first, followed by the needs of the family, and finally the needs of oneself. A commitment to the Lord and his commandments fosters selflessness. When two people love the Lord more than they love each other and love each other more than they love themselves, they can have a successful marriage.

A factor not included in the formula but which is just as important is fidelity and allegiance. We are commanded to cleave unto our spouses with our whole hearts; this expression leaves no room for sharing or dividing interest and love. Most specifically, this means no passionate relationships with others can be had while within the covenants of marriage, but this can also include obsessions, hobbies, work, and pornography. We must keep our covenants and the commandments in order to have a happy marriage.

QUOTES:

"The foundation for a happy and successful marriage is a marriage solemnized in the temple. To you who were married for time only, let me urge you to thoroughly investigate the blessings available to you by

going to the temple and having your family sealed to you for time and all eternity. Participating in these sacred ordinances should be your most important objective for achieving a successful marriage" (O. Leslie Stone, "Making Your Marriage Successful," *Ensign*, May 1978, 56).

"Complete trust in each other is one of the greatest enriching factors in marriage. Nothing devastates the core of mutual trust necessary to maintain a fulfilling relationship like infidelity. There is never a justification for adultery. Despite this destructive experience, occasionally marriages are saved and families preserved. To do so requires the aggrieved party to be capable of giving unreserved love great enough to forgive and forget. It requires the errant party to want desperately to repent and actually forsake evil" (James E. Faust, "The Enriching of Marriage," *Ensign*, Nov. 1977, 9).

"In a marriage, each of us is an individual. Each of us is different. There must be respect for differences, and although it is important and necessary that both the husband and the wife work to ameliorate those differences, there must be some recognition that they exist and that they are not necessarily undesirable. In fact, the difference may make the companionship more interesting" (Gordon B. Hinckley, *Stand a Little Taller*, Eagle Gate, Salt Lake City, Utah, 2001, 380).

NOTES:

Marriage brings greater possibilities for happiness than does any other human relationship. Yet some married couples fall short of their full potential. They let their romance become rusty, take each other for granted, allow other interests or clouds of neglect to obscure the vision of what their marriage really could be. Marriages would be happier if nurtured more carefully.

—Russell M. Nelson, "Nurturing Marriage," *Ensign*, May 2006.

Marriage brings greater possibilities for happiness than does any other human relationship. Yet some married couples fall short of their full potential. They let their romance become rusty, take each other for granted, allow other interests or clouds of neglect to obscure the vision of what their marriage really could be. Marriages would be happier if nurtured more carefully.

—Russell M. Nelson, "Nurturing Marriage," *Ensign*, May 2006.

Marriage brings greater possibilities for happiness than does any other human relationship. Yet some married couples fall short of their full potential. They let their romance become rusty, take each other for granted, allow other interests or clouds of neglect to obscure the vision of what their marriage really could be. Marriages would be happier if nurtured more carefully.

—Russell M. Nelson, "Nurturing Marriage," *Ensign*, May 2006.

Marriage brings greater possibilities for happiness than does any other human relationship. Yet some married couples fall short of their full potential. They let their romance become rusty, take each other for granted, allow other interests or clouds of neglect to obscure the vision of what their marriage really could be. Marriages would be happier if nurtured more carefully.

—Russell M. Nelson, "Nurturing Marriage," *Ensign*, May 2006.

LESSON NINETEEN

STRENGTHENING OUR FAMILIES

Hymns

No. 92, *"For the Beauty of the Earth"*
No. 294, *"Love at Home"*
No. 300, *"Families Can Be Together Forever"*

SUMMARY:

1. Not only are eternal marriages critical to the plan of salvation, but eternal families are also central to that plan. Heavenly Father organized families into units with a protective, loving father who provides for the family and a caring mother who teaches and nurtures the children. This unit is the basic organization of heaven. From the beginning, we as a church have strongly emphasized the importance of family life. We should be cautious of societal trends that downplay the blessings of a family. Families are the foundation for society. No other factor can repair society better than healthy families. We must continue to uphold our ideal of an eternal family.

2. Just as we build up reservoirs of food and emergency supplies for our families, we must also build up deep spiritual reservoirs for our children so they can fight through spiritual emergencies. These reservoirs should include prayer and scripture study habits, service opportunities, church attendance, and righteousness. We

should not be swayed by current trends to shift the responsibility to teaching our children character and competence from parents to outside sources, agencies, and institutions; the outside sources will never be as adequate as parents. More specifically, we should never allow the Church, as important as it is, to replace parents as the primary source children learn the gospel from. Instead, the Church should be a supporting influence through which activities and meetings can be scheduled and planned to focus on the family unit. We as parents need to remember that we set the example of truth and righteousness for our children.

3. Satan knows that attacking the family unit will result in the maximum amount of spiritual damage. We need to fortify our homes against evils such as divorce, abuse, and neglect. Parents can fight against these evils and strengthen their children with prayer, love, gospel teachings, and family scripture study. These practices help make the home a haven against outside temptations and influences. In the homes, reliance on the Lord should be constant and consistent. One of the best ways to establish and maintain this reliance is through daily prayer. We must have faith in our ability to really speak to our God and then receive His guidance on how to best protect our families. Parents can teach their children the gospel through scripture study and family home evening, and family counsel can be the venue where parents can organize the family and resolve disputes. Finally, we can safeguard our families by loving our children as God loves us. We must show them that love.

QUOTES:

"Brethren and sisters, material possessions and honors of the world do not endure. But your union as wife, husband, and family can. The only duration of family life that satisfies the loftiest longings of the human soul is forever. No sacrifice is too great to have the blessings of an eternal marriage. To qualify, one needs only to deny oneself of ungodliness and honor the ordinances of the temple. By making and keeping sacred temple covenants, we evidence our love for God, for our companion, and our real regard for our posterity—even those yet unborn. Our family is the focus of our greatest work and joy in this life; so will it be throughout all eternity, when we can 'inherit thrones, kingdoms, principalities, . . . powers, dominions, . . . exaltation and glory' (D&C 132:19)" (Russell M. Nelson, "Set in Order Thy House," *Ensign*, Nov. 2001, 71).

"If each and every one of us who are parents will reflect upon the responsibilities devolving upon us, we shall come to the conclusion that we should never permit ourselves to do anything that we are not willing to see our children do. We should set them an example that we wish them to imitate" (Journal of Discourses, 14:192).

"If we are to instill faith in our children, they must see us demonstrate our faith in their young lives. They must see us on our knees daily, asking the Lord for His blessings and expressing our gratitude unto Him. They need to see us using our priesthood to administer to those in need, and to bless our children. They need to see us reverently worshiping in our sacrament meetings. They need to see us cheerfully and willingly giving of our time and talents to the building of the Lord's kingdom here on earth. They need to see us proving our faith by the payment of our tithes and offerings to Him. They need to see us diligently studying and discussing the scriptures to increase our faith and understanding" (L. Tom Perry, "Train Up a Child," *Ensign*, May 1983, 78).

"One of our greatest goals as parents should be to enjoy the power and influence of the Holy Ghost in our homes" (Joseph B. Wirthlin, "The Unspeakable Gift," *Ensign*, May 2003, 28).

NOTES:

How Can I Unify
My Family?

How Can I Unify
My Family?

How Can I Unify
My Family?

How Can I Unify
My Family?

LESSON TWENTY

THE WOMEN
OF THE CHURCH

Hymns

No. 309, "As Sisters in Zion"
No. 293, "Each Life that Touches Ours for Good"
No. 310, "A Key Was Turned in Latter Days"

SUMMARY:

1. God loves all men and women equally. In the Church, this same equality exists across genders. Furthermore, this equality should be expected in an eternal marriage. However, the roles of men and women do differ. Women are given the responsibility to bear and raise children, and men have been given the responsibility to be fathers and to hold the priesthood. In the pre-mortal life, men and women were given equally challenging but equally diverse assignments and were also blessed with different abilities to accomplish these assignments. In the Church, we need to recognize these differences and treat both men and women with equal respect and reverence. The Relief Society is the Lord's organization for his daughters. This organization parallels the training the brethren receive through the priesthood. Men and women need to rely on each other to compliment the lessons and gifts they have respectively been given.

2. The Lord has always revered women. Being a righteous woman

in the last days is a noble calling to receive. Righteous women are responsible to save families and protect the home, which is the basic unit of society. This responsibility is a calling issued from the Lord in the pre-mortal life. Women can begin to fulfill this divine responsibility by ignoring societal trends and raising a family. Righteous women will find no greater satisfaction than they will when they fulfill this calling. Rest assured, however, all sisters who, through no fault of their own, are unable to be sealed in the temple to a worthy companion will still receive the blessings of an eternal family. Women who do not have this opportunity do not need to wait to begin fulfilling this responsibility They can still do much to help those around them and nurture those abilities and talents in preparation for having their own families.

3. This preparation should begin early. All girls should be taught that they are responsible for taking advantage of every opportunity to grow, receive light, and education. Each woman should prepare for raising families not only by practicing homemaking skills but also by preparing by becoming culturally refined and educated. Furthermore, each woman should be well versed in the scriptures so she can teach her children the gospel. Although this may seem old fashioned in today's society, no greater recognition can come to a woman than to be a daughter of God who is fulfilling her divine potential. Women who recognize this and live their lives accordingly will be a factor of major growth in the Church in the last days. These women will become examples to the world of how a true daughter of God should behave. We should all strive to fulfill our divine possibilities.

QUOTES:

"If we are constantly aware of the seeds of divinity in us, it will help us rise above earthly challenges and difficulties. Brigham Young said: 'When I look upon the faces of intelligent beings I look upon the image of the God I serve. There are none but what have a certain portion of divinity within them; and though we are clothed with bodies which are in the image of our God, yet this mortality shrinks before that portion of divinity which we inherit from our Father' (Discourses of Brigham Young, sel. John A. Widtsoe [1941], 168). Being aware of our divine heritage will help men young and old to grow and magnify the divinity which is within them and within all of us" (James E. Faust, "Them That Honour Me I Will Honour," *Ensign*, May 2001, 47).

"Nowhere does the doctrine of this Church declare that men are superior to women. Paul said to the Corinthians, 'Nevertheless neither is the man without the woman, neither the woman without the man, in the Lord' (1 Cor. 11:11). Each brings his or her own separate and unique strengths to the family and the Church. Women are not just cooks, stewards of our homes, or servants. They are much more. They are the enrichment of humanity" (James E. Faust, "The Highest Place of Honor," *Ensign*, May 1988, 36).

"Without you the plan could not function. Without you the entire program would be frustrated. As I have said before from this pulpit, when the process of creation occurred, Jehovah, the Creator, under instruction from His Father, first divided the light from the darkness and then separated the land from the waters. There followed the creation of plant life, followed by the creation of animal life. Then came the creation of man, and culminating that act of divinity came the crowning act, the creation of woman. Each of you is a daughter of God, endowed with a divine birthright. You need no defense of that position" (Gordon B. Hinckley, "Women of the Church," *Ensign*, Nov. 1996, 67).

NOTES:

YOU HAVE THE GIFT, THE OPPORTUNITY,
AND THE RESPONSIBILITY OF

doing good

YOU POSSESS AN INSTINCTIVE INCLINATION
TO HELP THOSE IN DISTRESS, AND YOU HAVE A
PECULIAR AND REMARKABLE WAY OF DOING SO.
THERE ARE SO MANY WHO NEED YOUR HELP.
—GORDON B. HINCKLEY, "TEN GIFTS FROM THE LORD," *ENSIGN*, NOV. 1985.

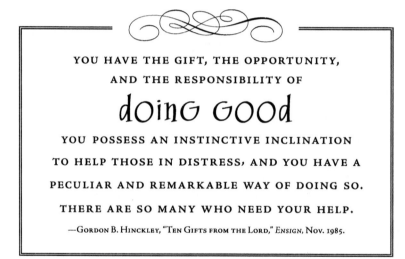

YOU HAVE THE GIFT, THE OPPORTUNITY,
AND THE RESPONSIBILITY OF

doing good

YOU POSSESS AN INSTINCTIVE INCLINATION
TO HELP THOSE IN DISTRESS, AND YOU HAVE A
PECULIAR AND REMARKABLE WAY OF DOING SO.
THERE ARE SO MANY WHO NEED YOUR HELP.
—GORDON B. HINCKLEY, "TEN GIFTS FROM THE LORD," *ENSIGN*, NOV. 1985.

YOU HAVE THE GIFT, THE OPPORTUNITY,
AND THE RESPONSIBILITY OF

doing good

YOU POSSESS AN INSTINCTIVE INCLINATION
TO HELP THOSE IN DISTRESS, AND YOU HAVE A
PECULIAR AND REMARKABLE WAY OF DOING SO.
THERE ARE SO MANY WHO NEED YOUR HELP.
—GORDON B. HINCKLEY, "TEN GIFTS FROM THE LORD," *ENSIGN*, NOV. 1985.

LESSON TWENTY-ONE

THE PROPHET
JOSEPH SMITH

Hymns

No. 27, *"Praise to the Man"*
No. 26, *"Joseph Smith's First Prayer"*
No. 19, *"We Thank Thee, O God, for a Prophet"*

SUMMARY:

1. Joseph Smith was foreordained to restore the gospel, to restore the priesthood, and to give hope to the world. He was prepared for and taught about this calling before the world was created. When Joseph Smith restored the gospel, hundreds of years had passed since the world had a prophet, and it was time to have authority and organization restored. The First Vision and the restoration of the gospel were planned by the Lord to be revealed at a specific time and in a specific country where He knew the gospel would flourish among His children.

2. God reveals Himself to men when appropriate and when that man or woman is prepared to receive Him and His Son Jesus Christ. The Lord prepared the Prophet Joseph to receive the First Vision. Joseph Smith was faithful and pure. He didn't have any preconceived notions or any bias. He also had faith that Heavenly Father would answer his prayer if he asked in faith. Furthermore, the timing of the First Vision was appropriate; the world was

covered in apostasy, and men were searching for the truth. Through the small and faithful prayer uttered by Joseph Smith, the Lord opened the heavens again. This vision was essential in dispelling the apostasy on the earth which was so great that nothing short of the First Vision would have restored the truth.

The First Vision taught several truths. First, we learned that God is a person of flesh and bone. Second, we learned that the Father and the Son are separate beings. Finally, through the Prophet Joseph, we learned that no church on the earth was the true church.

3. During the First Vision, Joseph Smith was told he would be the instrument that would restore the eternal gospel. Through him, priesthood power and authority were restored, the Book of Mormon was brought forth, and the organization of the Church was reinstated. These things were not restored all at once, but rather, they were restored piece by piece. Joseph Smith was first taught basic principles of the gospel such as baptism, and was later taught more complex doctrine such as sealing ordinances.

As members of the Church, we are familiar with the history of the Prophet Joseph. We understand the blessing and the truth he restored, and we also understand the pain and sorrow he suffered. Although he suffered persecution, he completed his mission to restore the gospel, and he sealed that truth and his testimony with his blood.

QUOTES:

"Joseph reported that he knew he must either put the Lord to the test and ask Him or perhaps choose to remain in darkness forever. Early one morning he stepped into a grove, now called sacred, and knelt and prayed, having faith that God would give him the enlightenment which he so earnestly sought. Two personages appeared to Joseph—the Father and the Son—and he was told, in answer to his question, that he was to join none of the churches, for none of them was true. The Prophet Joseph Smith taught us the principle of faith—by example. His simple prayer of faith on that spring morning in 1820 brought about this marvelous work which continues today throughout the world" (Thomas S. Monson, "The Prophet Joseph Smith: Teacher by Example," *Ensign*, Nov. 2005, 67).

"In bringing forth the Book of Mormon, young Joseph Smith learned line upon line the things he had to learn in order to become the prophet of the Restoration. Yet it is so that Joseph Smith's education continued past the translation and through his subsequent responsibilities and experiences" (James E. Faust, "Joseph Smith and the Book of Mormon," *Ensign*, Jan. 1996, 2).

"I bear solemn testimony of the divinity of Joseph Smith's call, of the magnitude of his accomplishments, of the virtue of his life, and of the security of his place among the great and honored of the Almighty in all generations of time. We stand in reverence before him. He is the great prophet of this dispensation. Let us not forget him. God be thanked for the Prophet Joseph" (Gordon B. Hinckley, *Stand a Little Taller*, Eagle Gate, Salt Lake City, Utah, 2001, 374).

NOTES:

JOSEPH SMITH, THE PROPHET AND SEER OF THE LORD, HAS DONE MORE, SAVE JESUS ONLY, FOR THE SALVATION OF MEN IN THIS WORLD, THAN ANY OTHER MAN THAT EVER LIVED IN IT. In the short space of twenty years, he has brought forth the Book of Mormon, which he translated by the gift and power of God, and has been the means of publishing it on two continents; has sent the fulness of the everlasting gospel, which it contained, to the four quarters of the earth; has brought forth the revelations and commandments which compose this book of Doctrine and Covenants, and many other wise documents and instructions for the benefit of the children of men; gathered many thousands of the Latter-day Saints, founded a great city, and left a fame and name that cannot be slain. He lived great, and he died great in the eyes of God and his people; and like most of the Lord's anointed in ancient times, has sealed his mission and his works with his own blood; and so has his brother Hyrum. In life they were not divided, and in death they were not separated!

— *D&C 135:3*

LESSON TWENTY-TWO

REVELATION:
"A CONTINUOUS MELODY
AND A THUNDEROUS
APPEAL"

Hymns

No. 143, *"Let the Holy Spirit Guide"*
No. 2, *"The Spirit of God"*
No. 149, *"As the Dew from Heaven Distilling"*

SUMMARY:

1. The Church maintains a firm position on the subject of revelation. We believe that not only does the Lord and His Son Jesus Christ communicate with men when it is appropriate, but we also believe that He is eager and willing to communicate with us. When we prepare ourselves for the experience of communing with God, He becomes approachable and knowable. This preparation cannot be completed through study alone. Neither can His gospel be understood through study alone. We must rely on revelation from God to understand His guidance and direction. The more we seek the Lord, the more He will reveal to us, and the greater our joy will be. God makes Himself available to us; we just need to seek Him and listen to His truths.

2. So many people, Latter-day Saints included, want their communications with God to be earth-shattering and spectacular. However, most revelation from the Lord comes through impressions and thoughts in the mind and heart. Revelation can take different

forms. Some revelations come in dreams, others through personal appearances, and still others through impressions in the mind. Examples of revelation are contained in the scriptures, and we can see the different ways God has communicated with His people in the past. We also learn what we can expect when we commune with the Lord and how to recognize the communication and revelation. Often, we don't recognize the revelations when they come to us; we should pray for a better understanding of revelations that we do receive, and we need to remember that although we may not recognize answers to our prayers, the Lord does hear and answer each and every one of them.

3. Possibly the most important aspect of revelation is the fact that continued revelation is received for the Church at large through the prophet. Revelation began when the Church was restored and often was given in the form of scripture. Through revelation, we have received the Doctrine and Covenants and the Pearl of Great Price. Furthermore, the Lord continues to direct and guide this gospel through revelation given to His chosen prophet. This revelation will not cease until faith ceases to exist on this earth. This faith is only one of the many requirements to receive revelation. We must also pray and fast so that we can receive revelation in our lives. Frequent and regular prayer with the Lord is the first step in drawing close enough to the Spirit to receive revelation. The Lord is eager to commune with us, we just have to draw near to Him and listen to what He has to say to us. Often, we forget to meditate after our daily prayers; we should refrain from forgetting this crucial step in receiving revelation. The Lord will answer our questions if we ask in faith and listen for His voice.

QUOTES:

"The patterns of revelation are not dramatic. The voice of inspiration is a still voice, a small voice. There need be no trance, no sanctimonious declaration. It is quieter and simpler than that" (Boyd K. Packer, "Revelation in a Changing World," *Ensign*, Nov. 1989, 14).

"It is my firm belief that the bishop of every ward and the president of every stake have the right to receive revelation as to what is best for their ward and stake members. Also, that every person who accepts a calling from the Lord has the right to receive revelation in connection with that calling if he is living righteously so that he is in tune with the Spirit of the Lord" (Henry D. Taylor, "Revelation," *Ensign*, May 1978, 38).

"Test divine revelation. Hear the voice of the Lord. It is real; it is personal; it is true. Reason does not and cannot replace revelation" (Charles Didier, "Man's Search for Divine Truth," *Ensign*, Nov. 2005, 48).

NOTES:

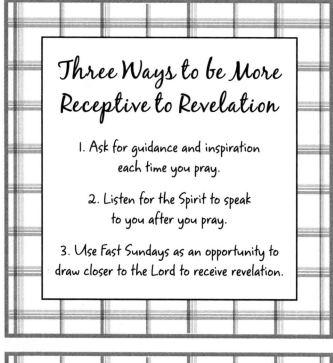

Three Ways to be More Receptive to Revelation

1. Ask for guidance and inspiration each time you pray.

2. Listen for the Spirit to speak to you after you pray.

3. Use Fast Sundays as an opportunity to draw closer to the Lord to receive revelation.

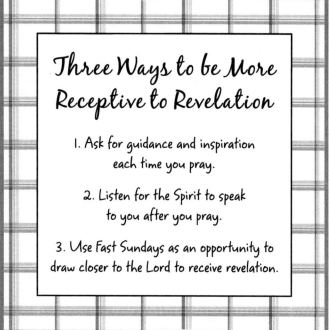

Three Ways to be More Receptive to Revelation

1. Ask for guidance and inspiration each time you pray.

2. Listen for the Spirit to speak to you after you pray.

3. Use Fast Sundays as an opportunity to draw closer to the Lord to receive revelation.

LESSON TWENTY-THREE

SHEPHERDS
OF THE FLOCK

Hymns

No. 21, "Come, Listen to a Prophet's Voice"
No. 19, "We Thank Thee, O God, for a Prophet"
No. 24, "God Bless Our Prophet Dear"

SUMMARY:

1. Contrary to rumors that persist in society about the Church, Jesus Christ is the head of the Church and directs the work through His appointed prophets. The Church is organized with a Prophet, Apostles, and other General Authorities. Furthermore, local leaders have been appointed and sustained to make sure each member of the Church has access to the holy Melchizedek Priesthood. Each leader is divinely called and set apart to receive revelation for the members they preside over. Not one leader who has been called has been perfect, but they are still called of the Lord and we should uphold and sustain them to the best of our abilities. These men who are called are our protection against the adversary, and we will not be led astray if we observe their counsel.

2. In general conferences and other opportunities when the General Authorities speak to the members of the Church, similar messages are heard. This is because each prophet faces similar challenges and problems, and even more so, the solution to these problems has not

changed. The gospel of Christ has always taught and will always teach one way to abstain from sin and return to our Heavenly Father. Regardless of the situation one faces, direction from the brethren will always come from the same truths. Unfortunately, prophets are not always listened to, and their counsel is not always followed. Often in the Church, we have the tendency to ignore our current prophet and take counsel from prophets of an earlier day. Nothing could be more dangerous. When the world ceases to listen to its prophet, it ceases to progress. Prophets are not looking for popularity; they are looking to serve the Lord and His people. Often, they are rejected by society because the prophets first reject immoral behavior that society often upholds. We cannot afford to be so careless.

3. As always, we as parents have a responsibility to teach our children to sustain and follow our Church leaders. The best way to teach them this principle is to sustain and follow our Church leaders ourselves. Our children will learn the respect and revere these leaders through our examples. Teach your children to pray for church leaders, to speak well of them, and to follow their examples. This lesson is imperative for us and our children to learn. When we follow the instruction of our leaders, we find safety and peace. The Lord has placed safeguards against the leaders of this Church from leading it astray. If we follow their guidance, we will be able to avoid sin, and we will draw closer to eternal life.

QUOTES:

"I believe that never before in the history of the Church has there been more unity than exists among my Brethren of the First Presidency, the Quorum of the Twelve, and the other General Authorities of the Church, who have been called and chosen and who are now guiding the Church. I believe there is ample evidence of this. The present leadership of God's earthly kingdom has enjoyed the Savior's guiding inspiration longer than any other group. We are the oldest group ever to lead the Church. My association with some of these men for almost half a century qualifies me, I think, to state with confidence that my Brethren, without exception, are good, honorable, and trustworthy men. I know their hearts. They are the servants of the Lord. Their only desire is to labor in their great callings and build up the kingdom of God on earth. Our Brethren who are serving in this day and time are proven, tried, and true. Some are not as physically strong as they used to be, but their hearts are so pure, their experience so great, their minds so sharp, and their spiritual wisdom so deep that it is a comfort just to be in their presence" (James E. Faust, "Called and Chosen," *Ensign*, Nov. 2005, 53).

"If we listen to the prophets of this day, poverty would be replaced with loving care for the poor and needy. Many serious and deadly health problems would be avoided through compliance with the Word of Wisdom and the laws of sexual purity. Payment of tithing would bless us and we would have sufficient for our needs. If we follow the counsel given by the prophets, we can have a life in mortality where we do not bring upon ourselves unnecessary pain and self-destruction. This does not mean we will not have challenges. We will. This does not mean we will not be tested. We will, for this is part of our purpose on earth. But if we will listen to the counsel of our prophet, we will become stronger and be able to withstand the tests of mortality. We will have hope and joy. All the words of counsel from the prophets of all generations have been given so that we may be strengthened and then be able to lift and strengthen others" (Robert D. Hales, "Hear the Prophet's Voice and Obey," *Ensign*, May 1995, 17).

"We also need to support and sustain our local leaders, because they also have been 'called and chosen.' Every member of this Church may receive counsel from a bishop or a branch president, a stake or a mission president, and the President of the Church and his associates. None of these brethren asked for his calling. None is perfect. Yet they are the servants of the Lord, called by Him through those entitled to inspiration. Those called, sustained, and set apart are entitled to our sustaining support" (James E. Faust, "Called and Chosen," *Ensign*, Nov. 2005, 53).

NOTES:

LISTEN
to a prophet's voice
AND OBEY.
There is safety in following the living prophet.

—*Robert D. Hales, "Hear the Prophet's Voice and Obey,"* Ensign, *May 1995.*

LISTEN
to a prophet's voice
AND OBEY.
There is safety in following the living prophet.

—*Robert D. Hales, "Hear the Prophet's Voice and Obey,"* Ensign, *May 1995.*

LISTEN
to a prophet's voice
AND OBEY.
There is safety in following the living prophet.

—*Robert D. Hales, "Hear the Prophet's Voice and Obey,"* Ensign, *May 1995.*

LISTEN
to a prophet's voice
AND OBEY.
There is safety in following the living prophet.

—*Robert D. Hales, "Hear the Prophet's Voice and Obey,"* Ensign, *May 1995.*

LISTEN
to a prophet's voice
AND OBEY.
There is safety in following the living prophet.

—*Robert D. Hales, "Hear the Prophet's Voice and Obey,"* Ensign, *May 1995.*

LISTEN
to a prophet's voice
AND OBEY.
There is safety in following the living prophet.

—*Robert D. Hales, "Hear the Prophet's Voice and Obey,"* Ensign, *May 1995.*

LISTEN
to a prophet's voice
AND OBEY.
There is safety in following the living prophet.

—*Robert D. Hales, "Hear the Prophet's Voice and Obey,"* Ensign, *May 1995.*

LISTEN
to a prophet's voice
AND OBEY.
There is safety in following the living prophet.

—*Robert D. Hales, "Hear the Prophet's Voice and Obey,"* Ensign, *May 1995.*

LISTEN
to a prophet's voice
AND OBEY.
There is safety in following the living prophet.

—*Robert D. Hales, "Hear the Prophet's Voice and Obey,"* Ensign, *May 1995.*

LESSON TWENTY-FOUR

SHARING THE GOSPEL

Hymns

No. 249, *"Called to Serve"*
No. 251, *"Behold! A Royal Army"*
No. 84, *"Faith of Our Fathers"*

SUMMARY:

1. Missionary work is moving and rewarding. Hours of missionary work are completely satisfying as souls embrace the gospel of Jesus Christ and are baptized. Sharing the gospel not only touches the lives of converts and their families, but it also brings peace and joy into our lives. The Lord has promised us blessings if we boldly share the gospel. He has promised us additional help from the Spirit and from the other side of the veil, and he has promised us that are sins will be more readily forgiven if we consistently share His gospel with others. We do not have to be set apart as a full-time missionary to preach the gospel. Every member can be a missionary and has the obligation and the calling to spread the gospel to those around him or her. The Lord will help us with this task as long as we are sacrificing to do what we can to bring souls unto Him.

2. We need not go out of our way to find people to teach. The Lord places people in our lives with whom we can share the gospel. First,

we need to start by fellowshipping these people, and we need to be good examples. Then, we must pray to the Lord and ask for His guidance on how to best share the gospel with those who are ready. We should also ask for help in identifying those He has prepared for us to share the gospel with. However, receiving this guidance does not guarantee that someone we share the gospel with will be baptized. This should not discourage us.

Missionary work does not just include teaching the gospel to those around us. It also includes fellowshipping new converts and less-active members in our ward. Fellowshipping can be the best deterrent of inactivity. We should actively include new members and members coming back into activity in our meetings, where appropriate, and in our auxiliary activities. Furthermore, we should ensure that these members are regularly being home taught and visiting teachers who fulfill that responsibility.

3. We can also foster missionary work within our own families. We should teach our children that missionary work is a blessing from the Lord. Furthermore, we should teach our young men that serving a mission is required. Parents can help their young men understand the standards for missionaries through example and prayer. We can teach them the importance of missionary work by consistently praying for the missionaries, helping them save for a mission, and allowing them to witness your missionary work. We must teach them from a very young age and plant the seed of missionary work in their minds so there is no question as to whether they will serve a mission when they are of age. In addition, we need to understand the importance of couple missionaries. We are not released from our responsibility to share the gospel as we get older; we still have the same responsibility, and in many cases where health and other conditions allow us, we have the time to commit to a full-time mission. We cannot overlook our senior couples as a great missionary resource.

QUOTES:

"We are missionaries every day in our families, in our schools, in our places of employment, and in our communities. Regardless of our age, experience, or station in life, we are all missionaries" (David A. Bednar, "Becoming a Missionary," *Ensign*, Nov. 2005, 44).

"Every one of you [teachers and priests] should be given the assignment to home teach with a companion who holds the Melchizedek Priesthood. What an opportunity to prepare for a mission. What a privilege to learn the discipline of duty. A young man will automatically turn from concern for self when he is assigned to 'watch over' others (D&C 20:53)" (Thomas S. Monson, "Do Your Duty—That Is Best," *Ensign*, Nov. 2005, 57).

NOTES:

IDENTIFY THREE
MISSIONARY OPPORTUNITIES
AND SET GOALS TO
ACCOMPLISH THEM

1. _____
_____
_____ GOAL: _____

2. _____
_____
_____ GOAL: _____

3. _____
_____
_____ GOAL: _____

IDENTIFY THREE
MISSIONARY OPPORTUNITIES
AND SET GOALS TO
ACCOMPLISH THEM

1. _____
_____
_____ GOAL: _____

2. _____
_____
_____ GOAL: _____

3. _____
_____
_____ GOAL: _____

IDENTIFY THREE
MISSIONARY OPPORTUNITIES
AND SET GOALS TO
ACCOMPLISH THEM

1. _____
_____
_____ GOAL: _____

2. _____
_____
_____ GOAL: _____

3. _____
_____
_____ GOAL: _____

IDENTIFY THREE
MISSIONARY OPPORTUNITIES
AND SET GOALS TO
ACCOMPLISH THEM

1. _____
_____
_____ GOAL: _____

2. _____
_____
_____ GOAL: _____

3. _____
_____
_____ GOAL: _____

ABOUT THE AUTHOR

Kimberly Shaffer graduated from Brigham Young University with a bachelor's degree in marriage, family, and human development. She resides in Manhattan, Kansas, and is pursuing a master's degree in landscape architecture. She is the author of *The Ready Resource for Relief Society Volume One*.